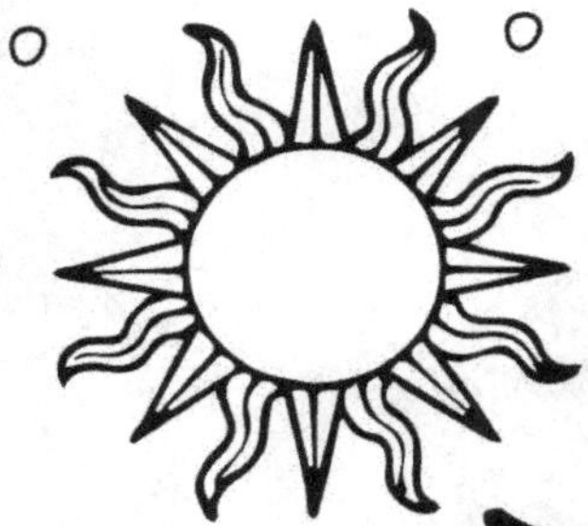

This book

Belongs to

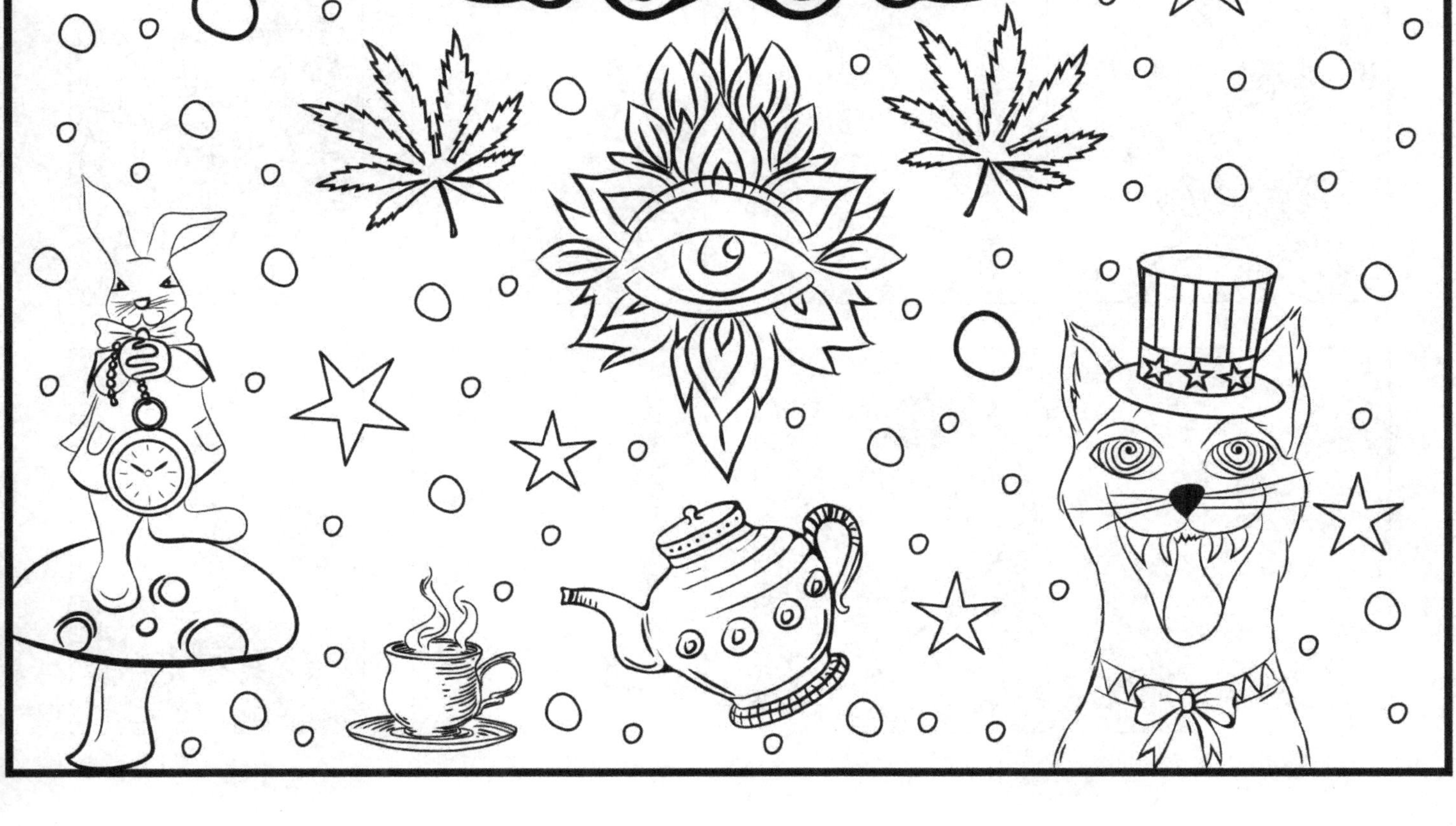

Contents

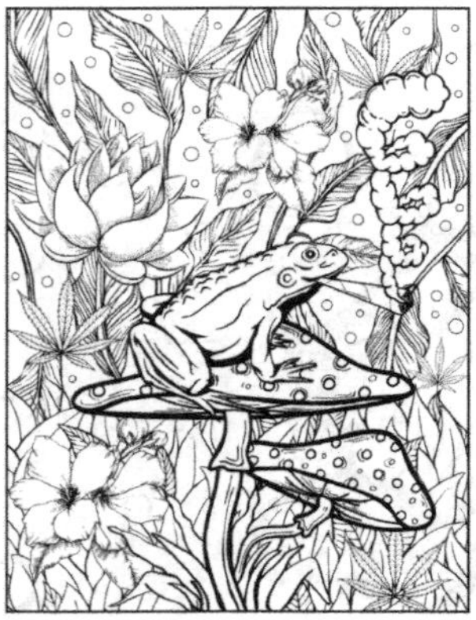
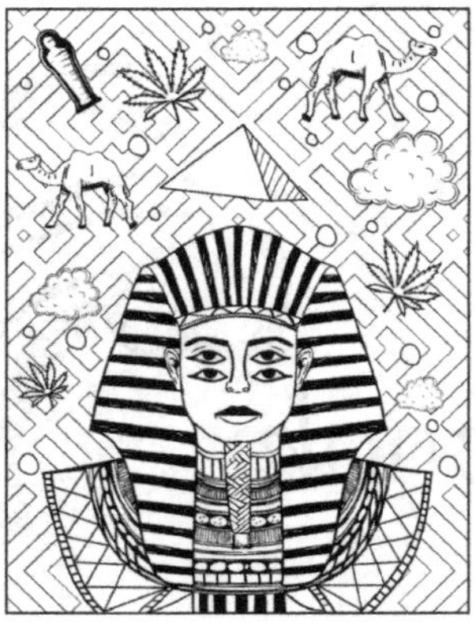
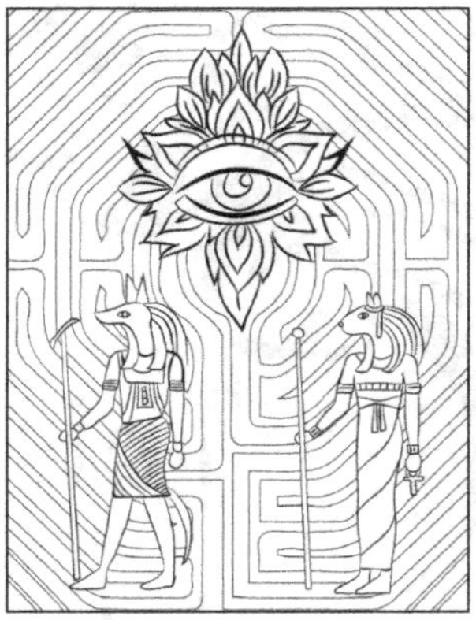
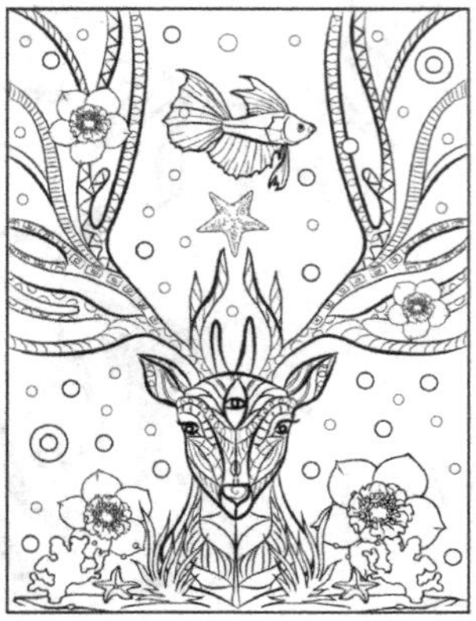
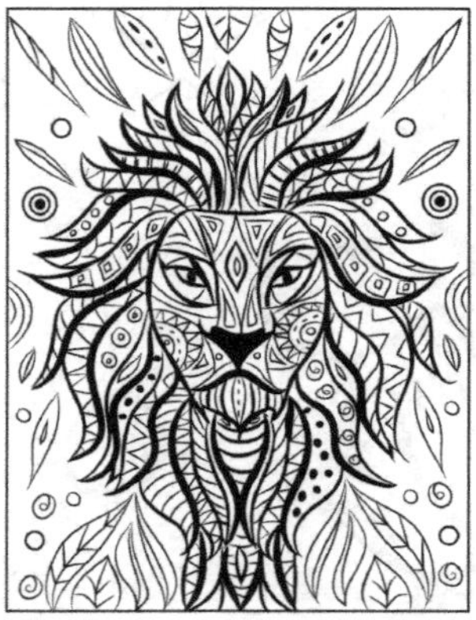
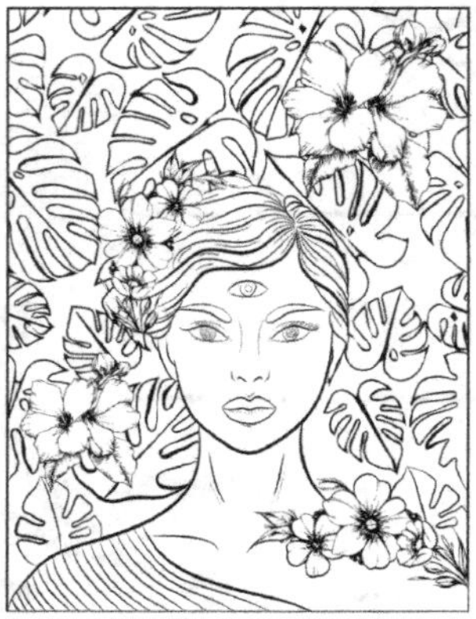
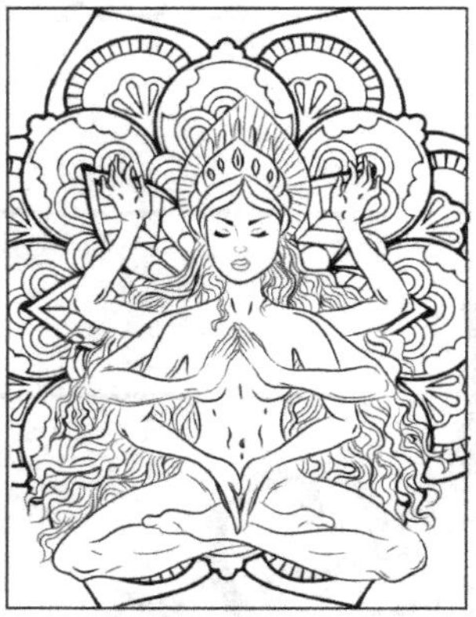
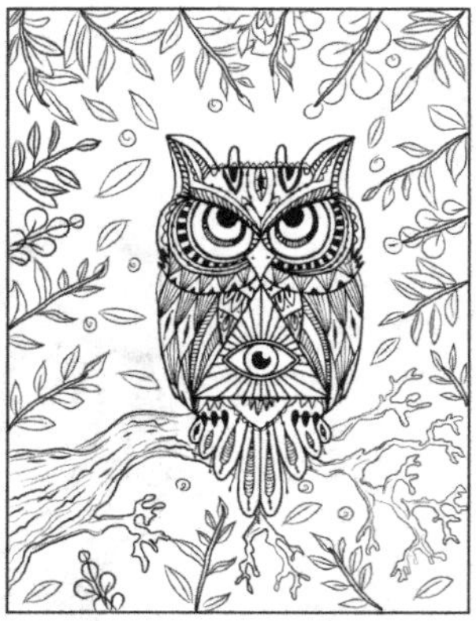
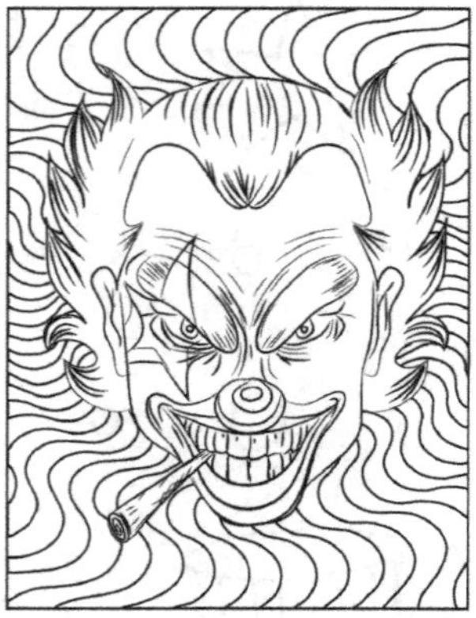
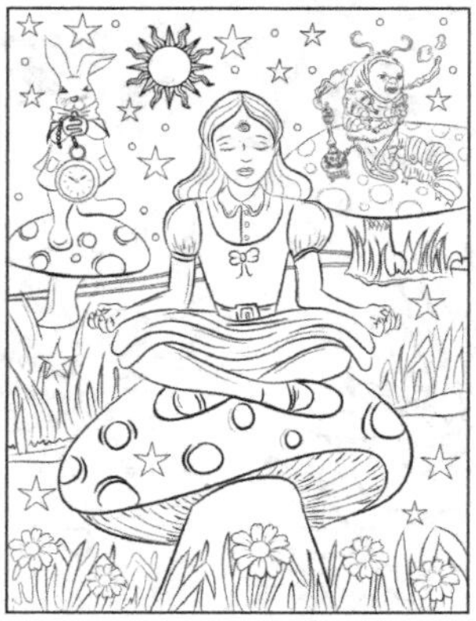
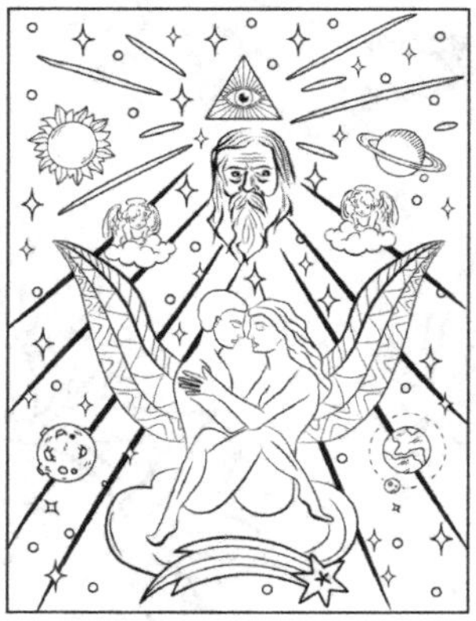
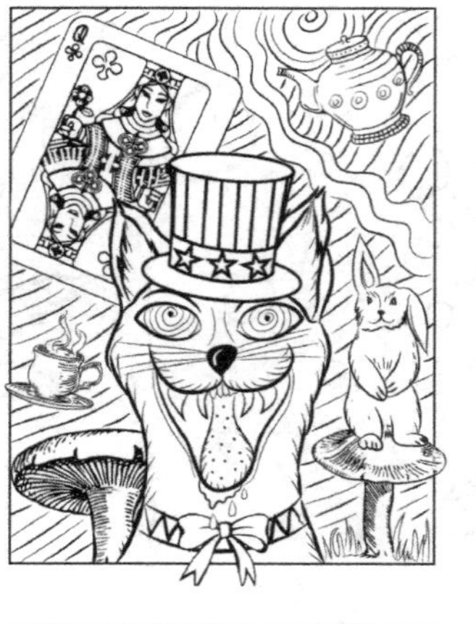
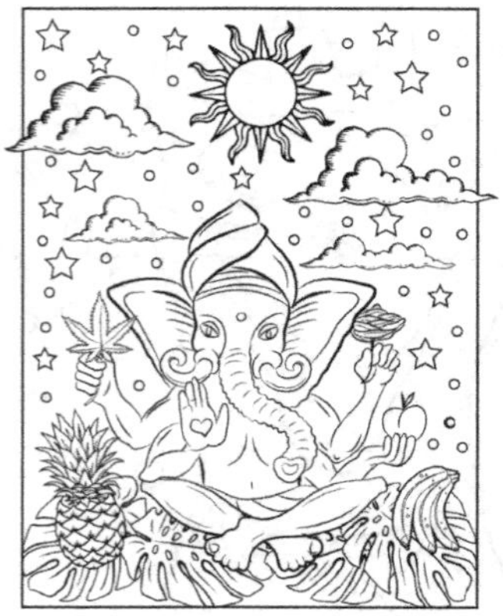
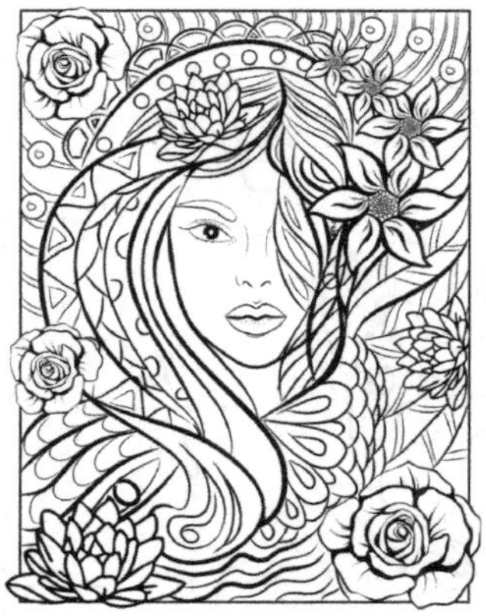
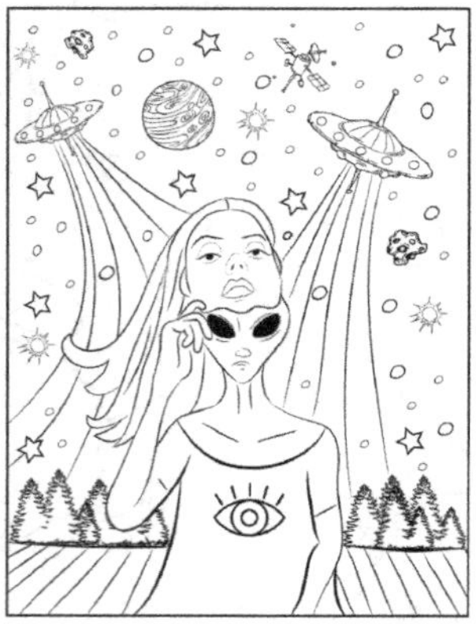
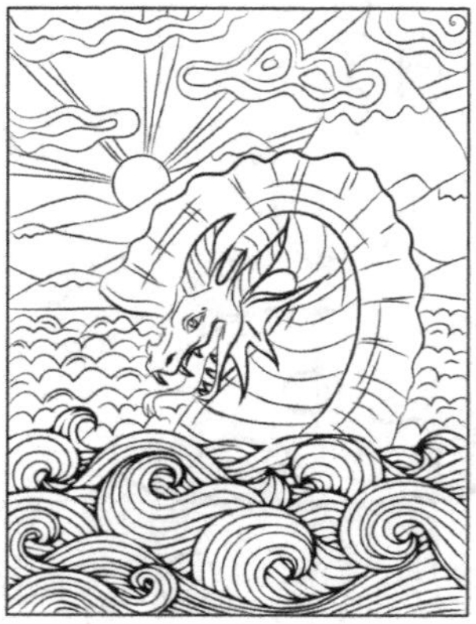

Contents

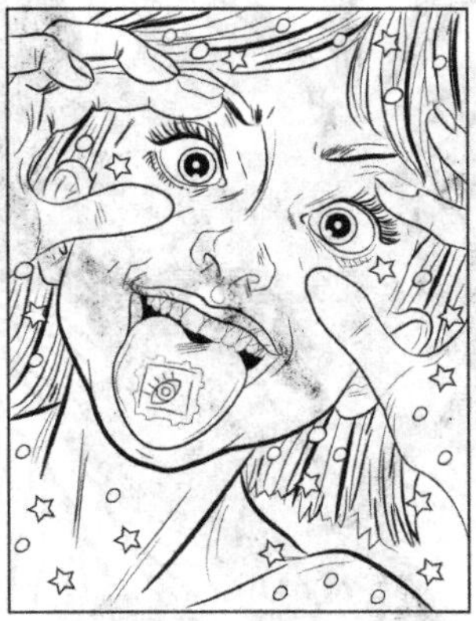
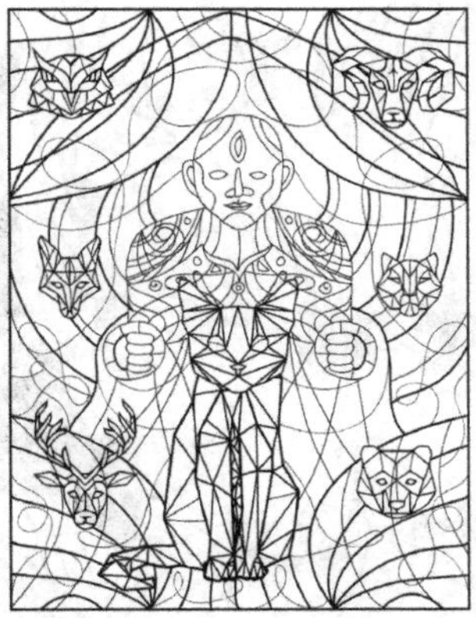
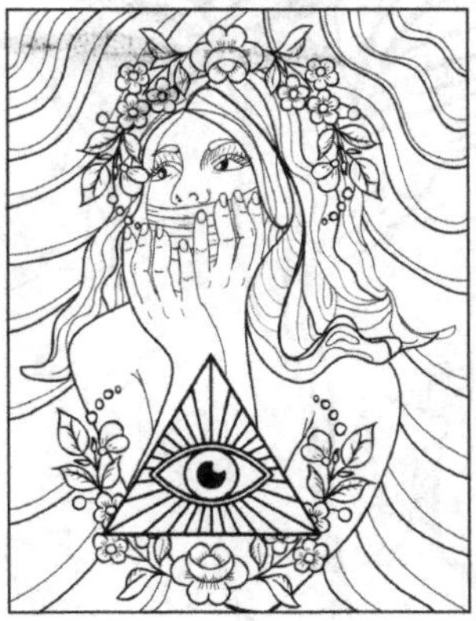
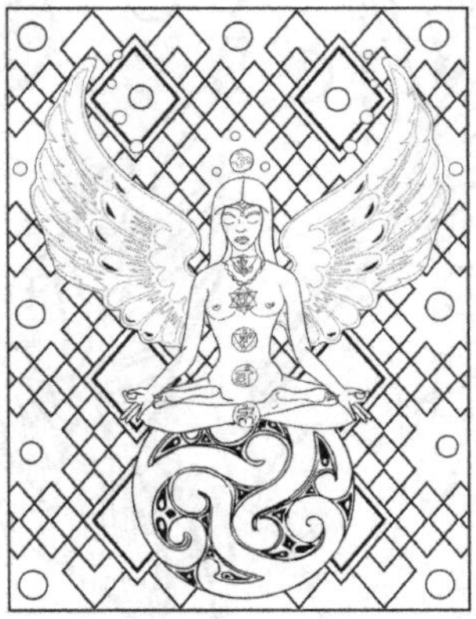
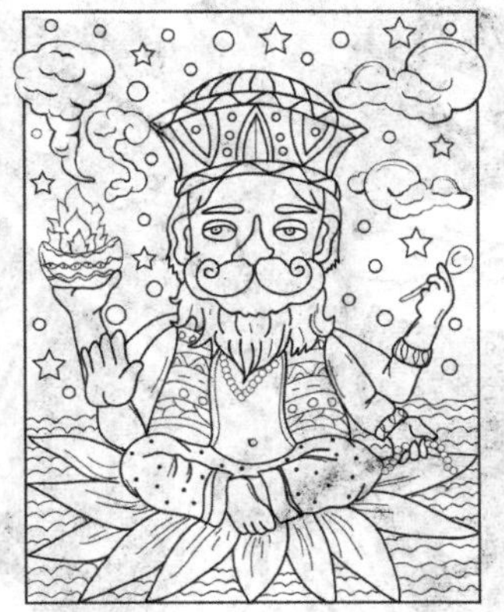
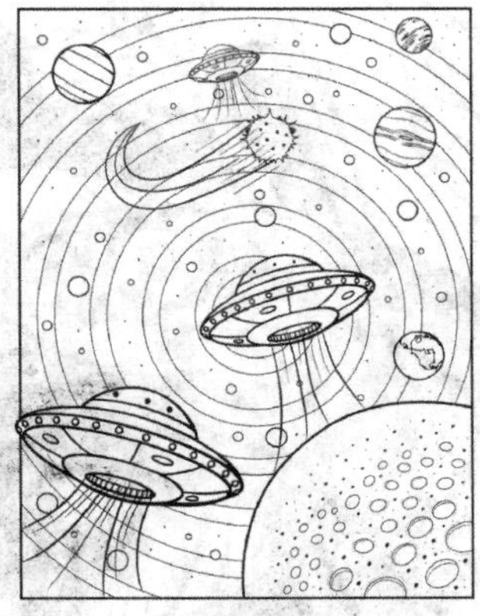
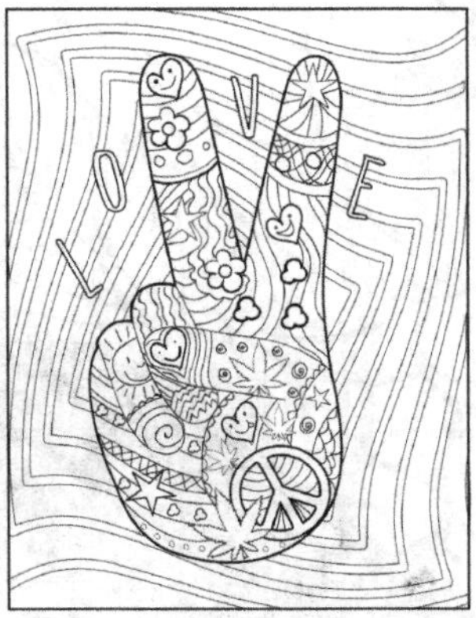

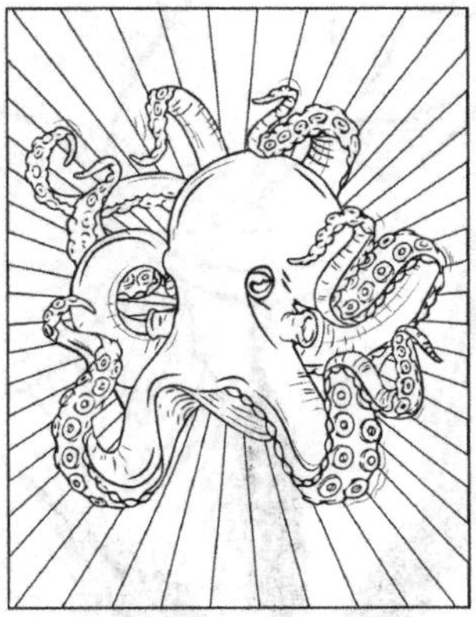
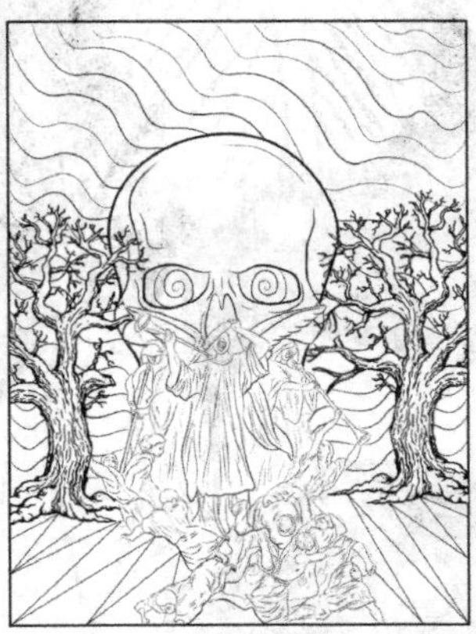
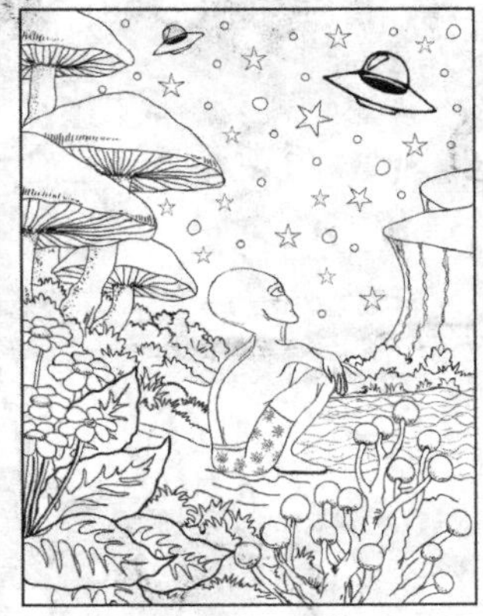
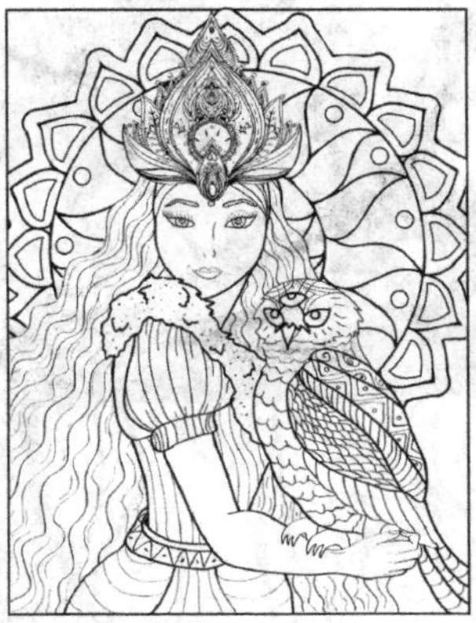
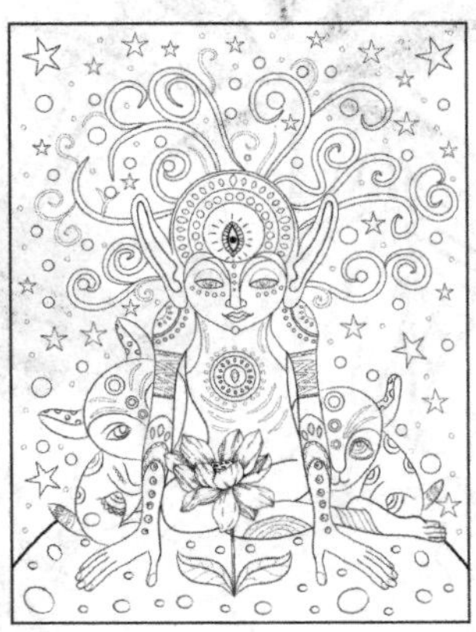
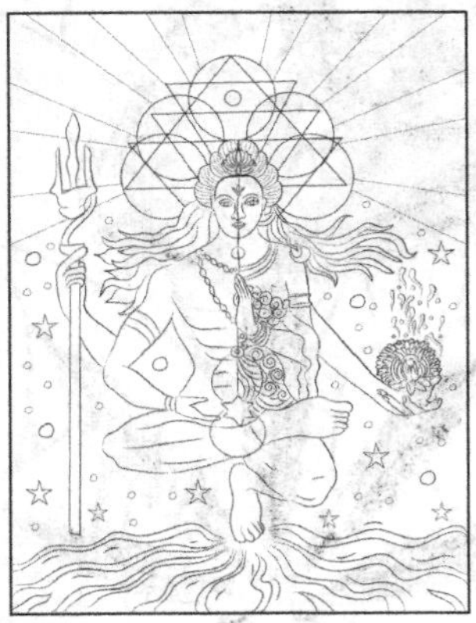
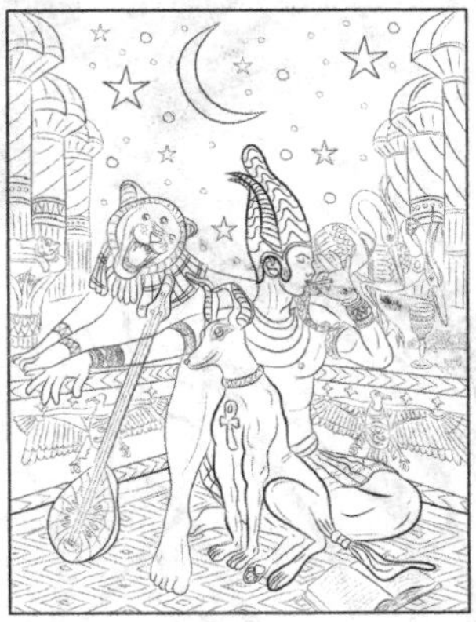
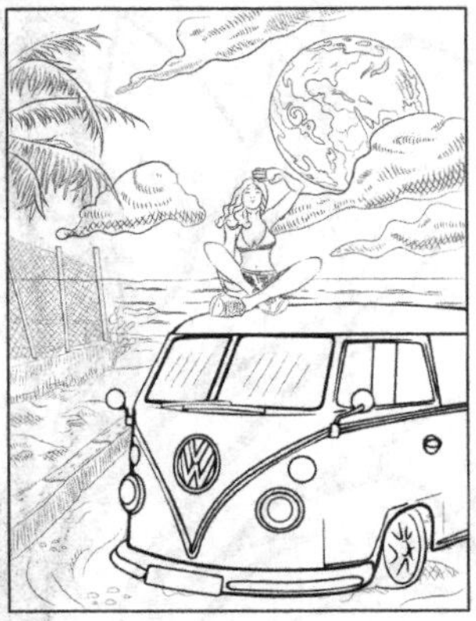
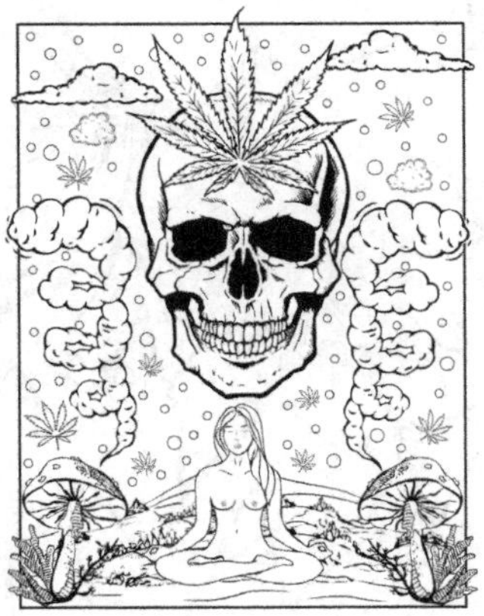

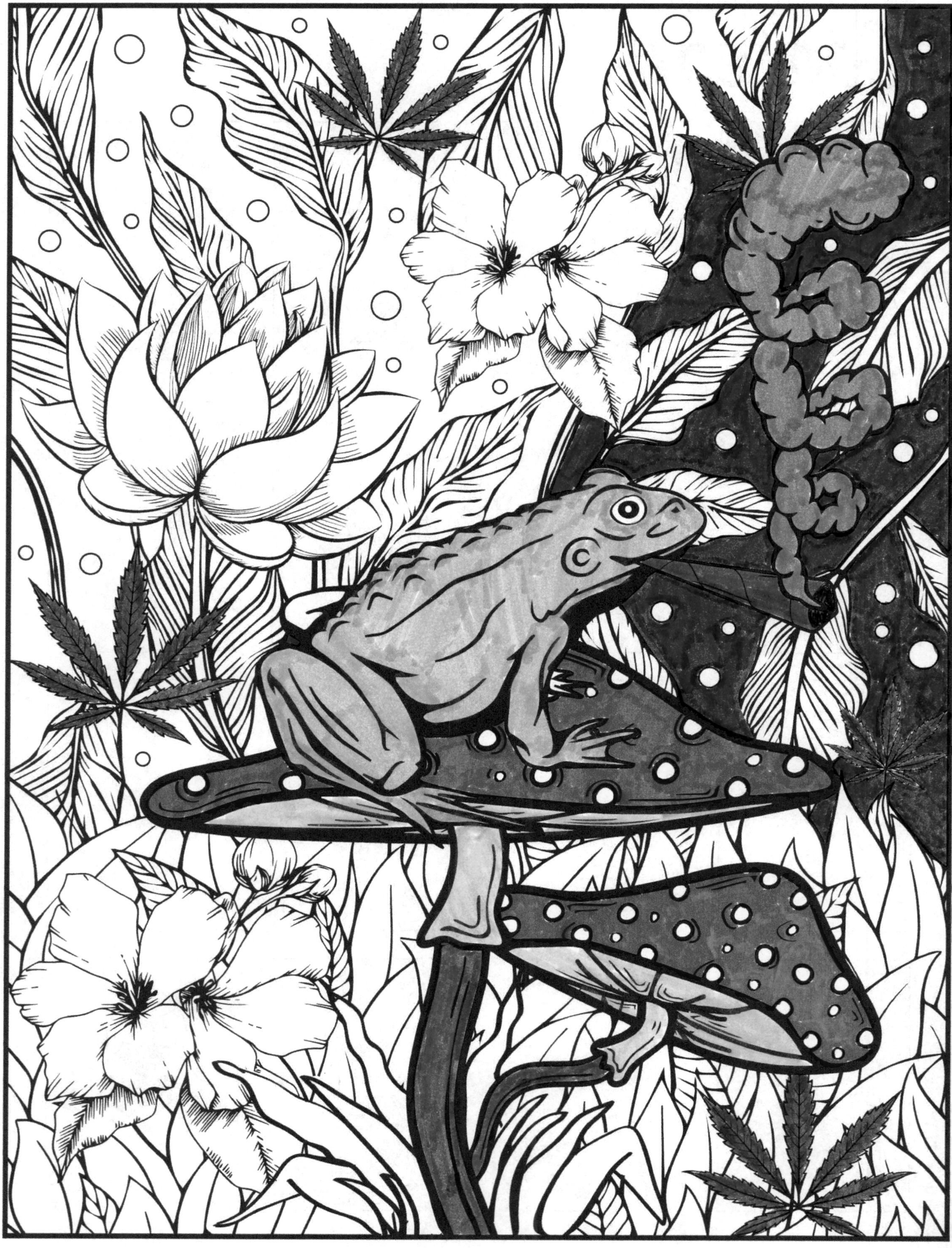

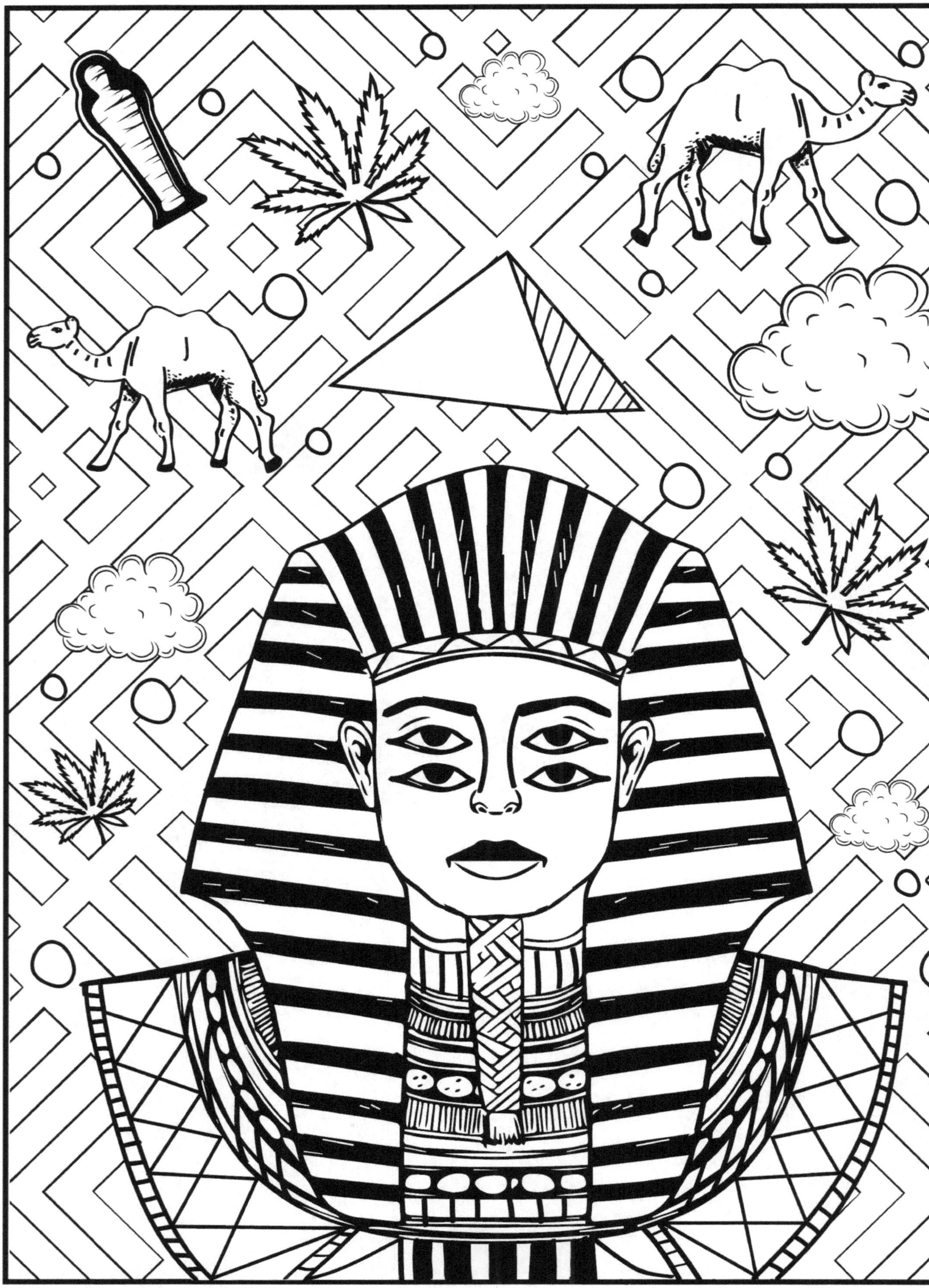

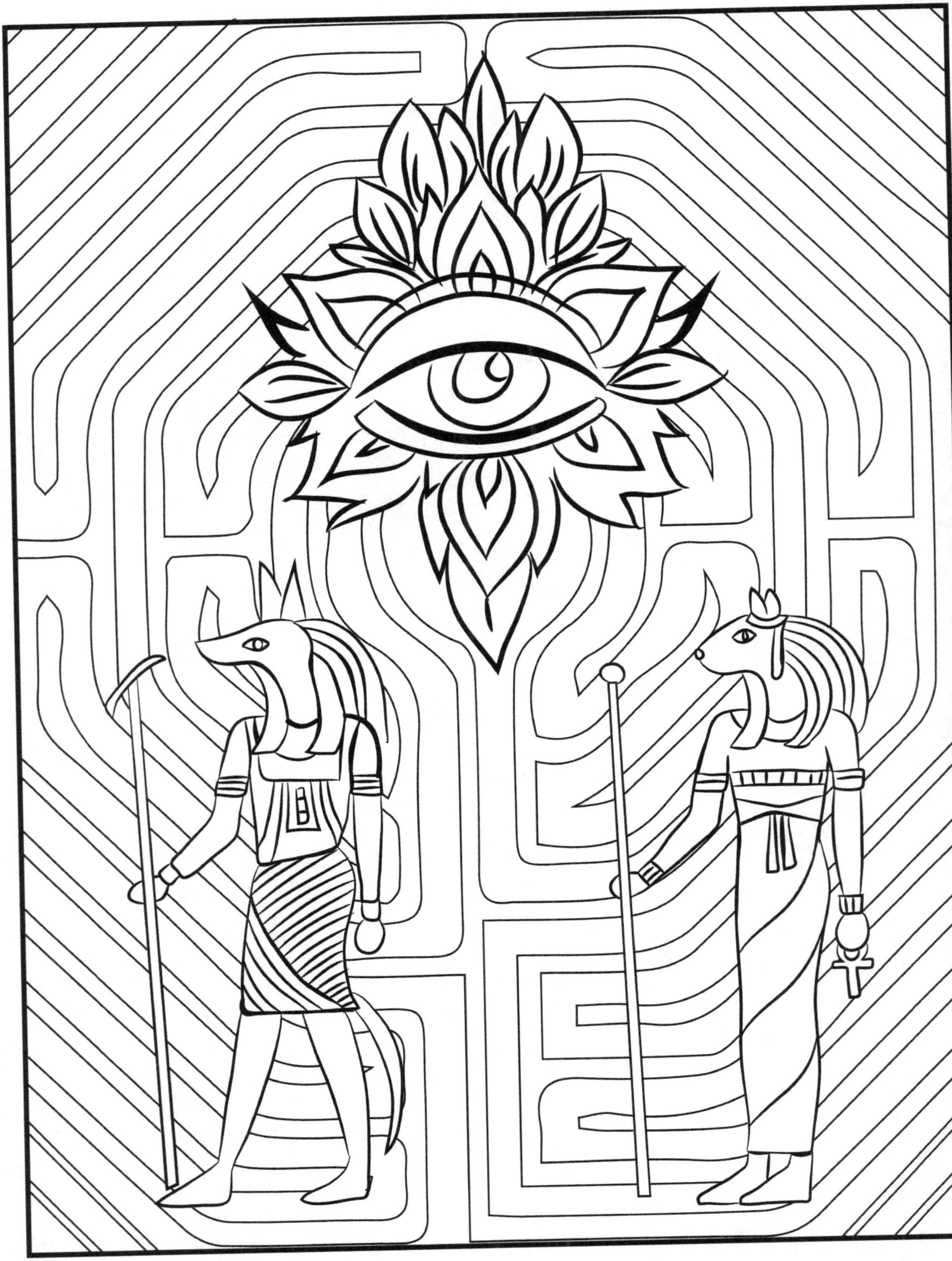

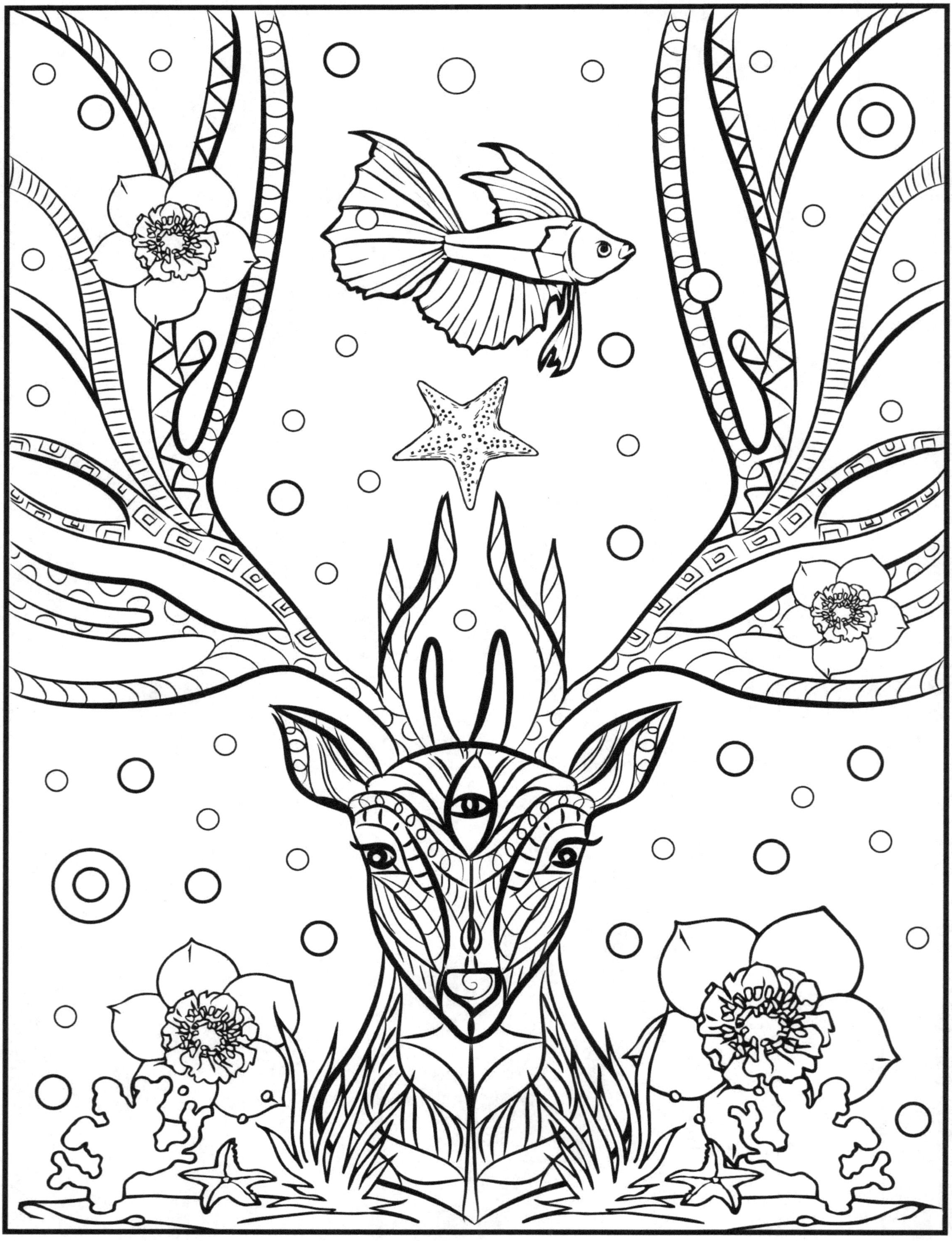

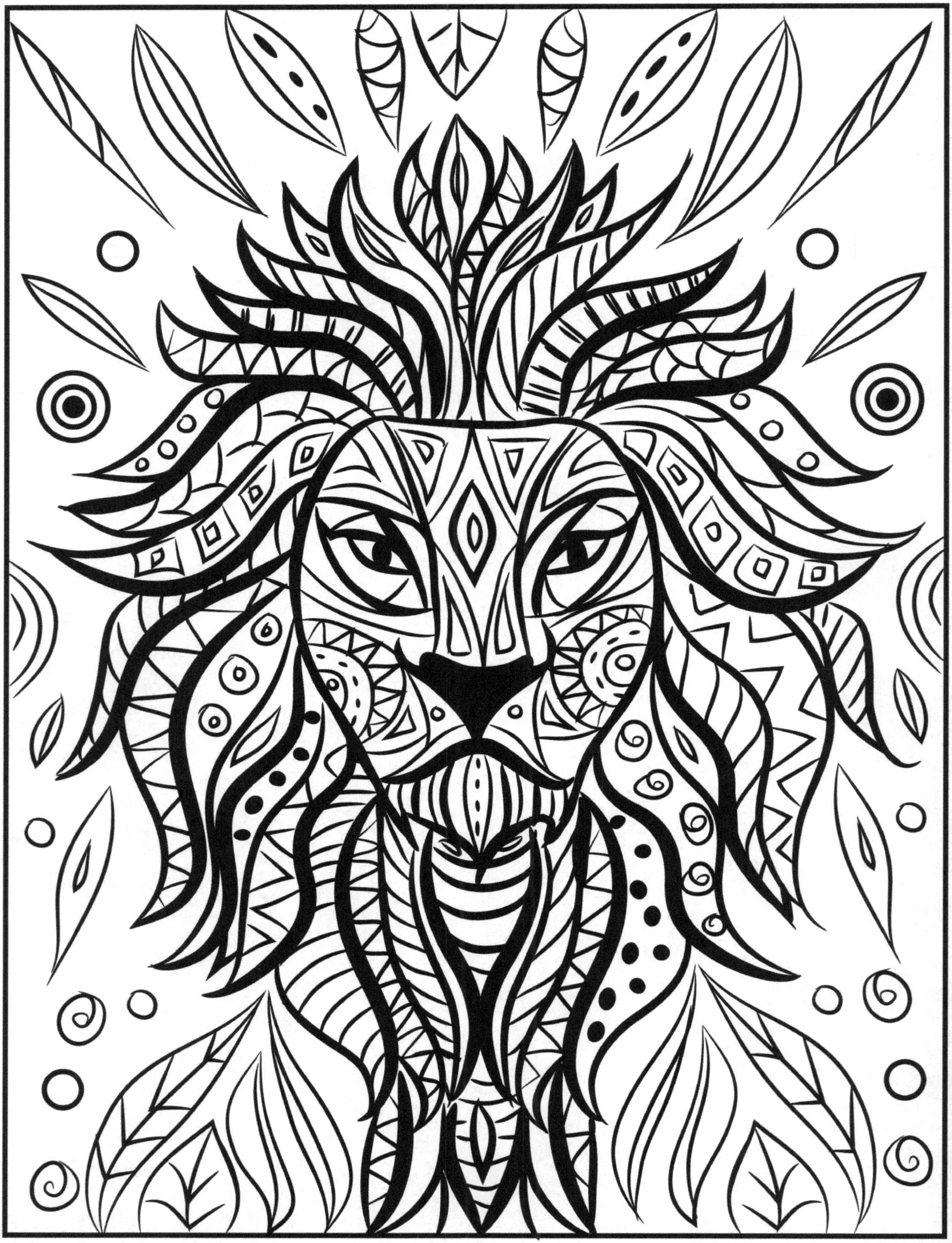

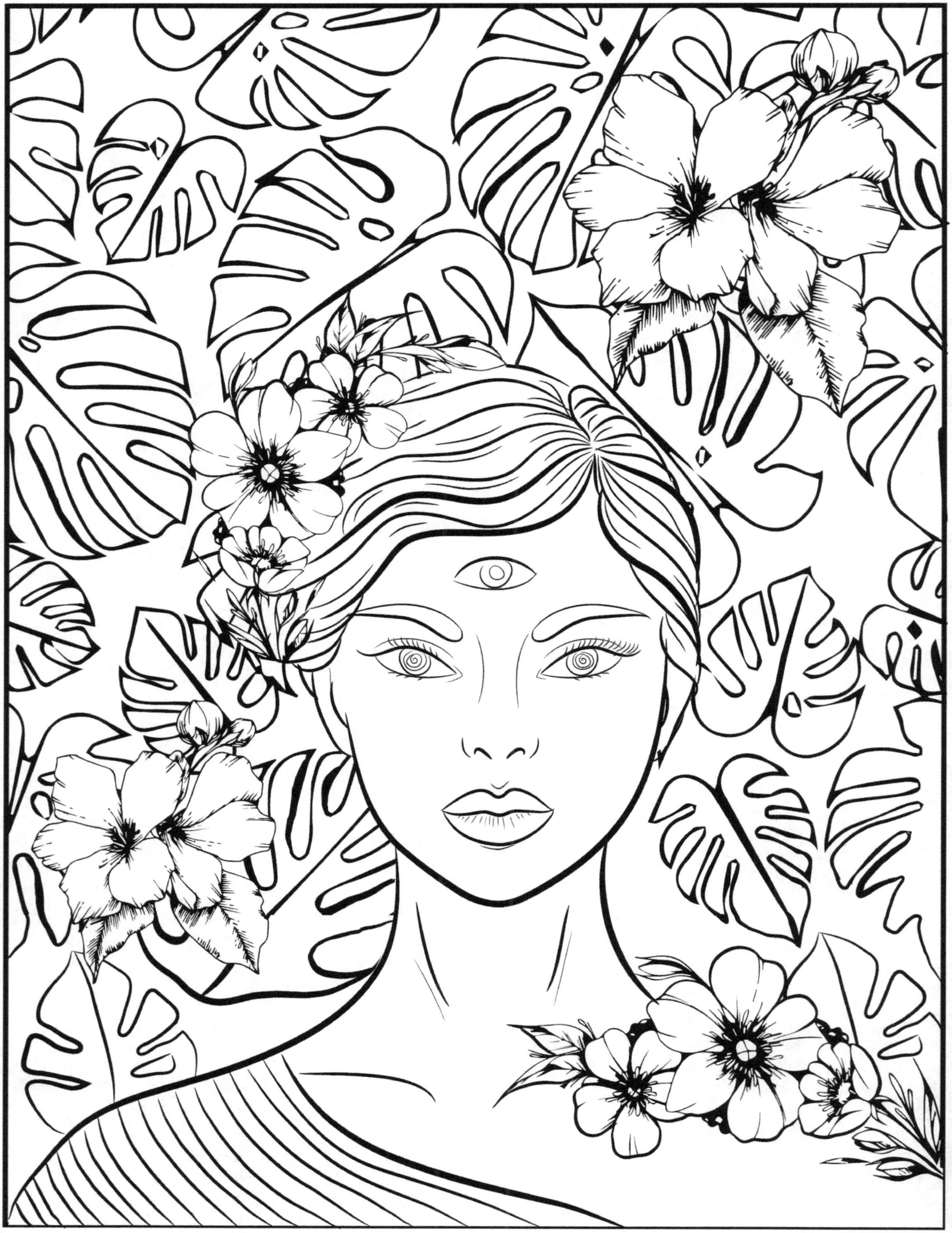

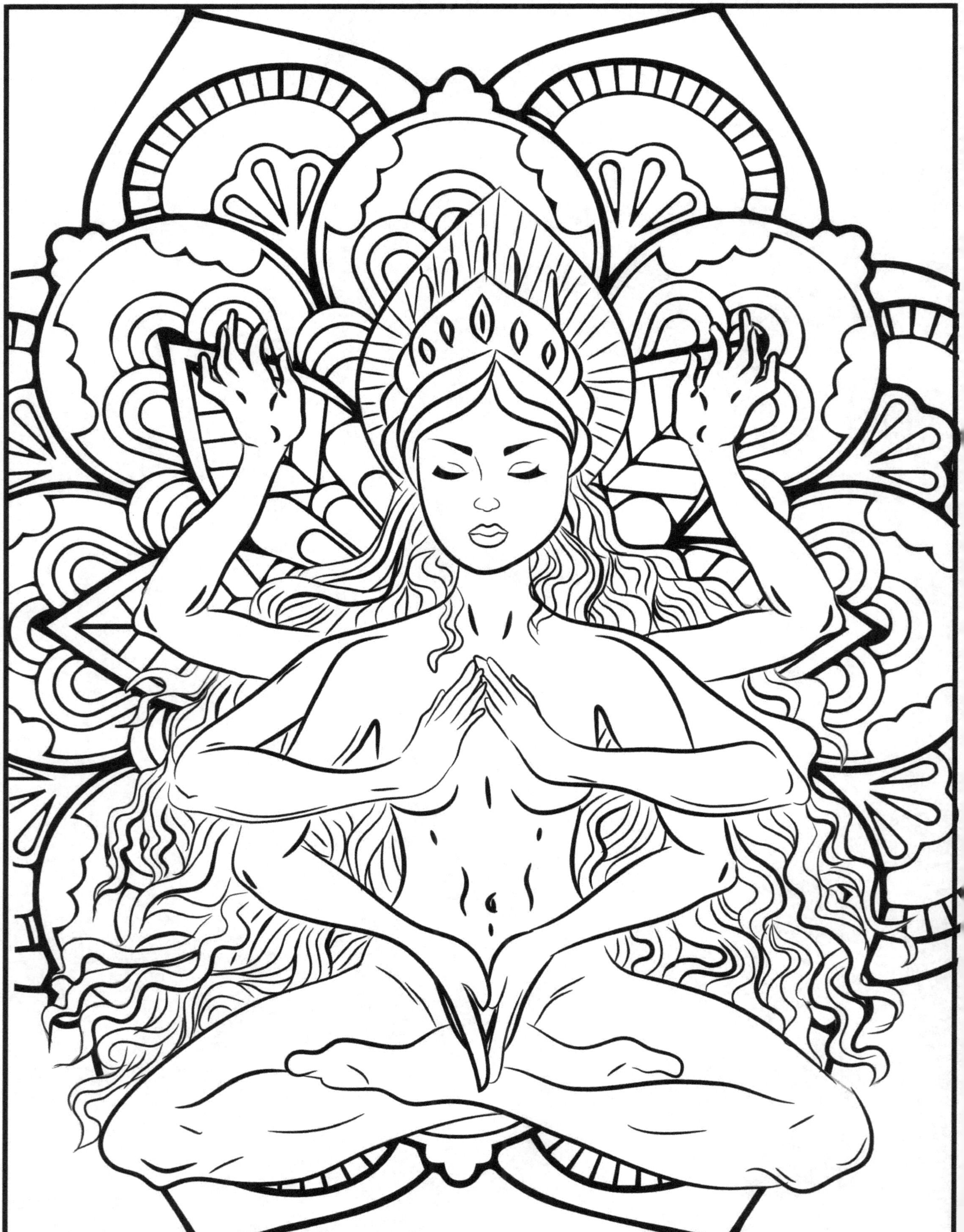

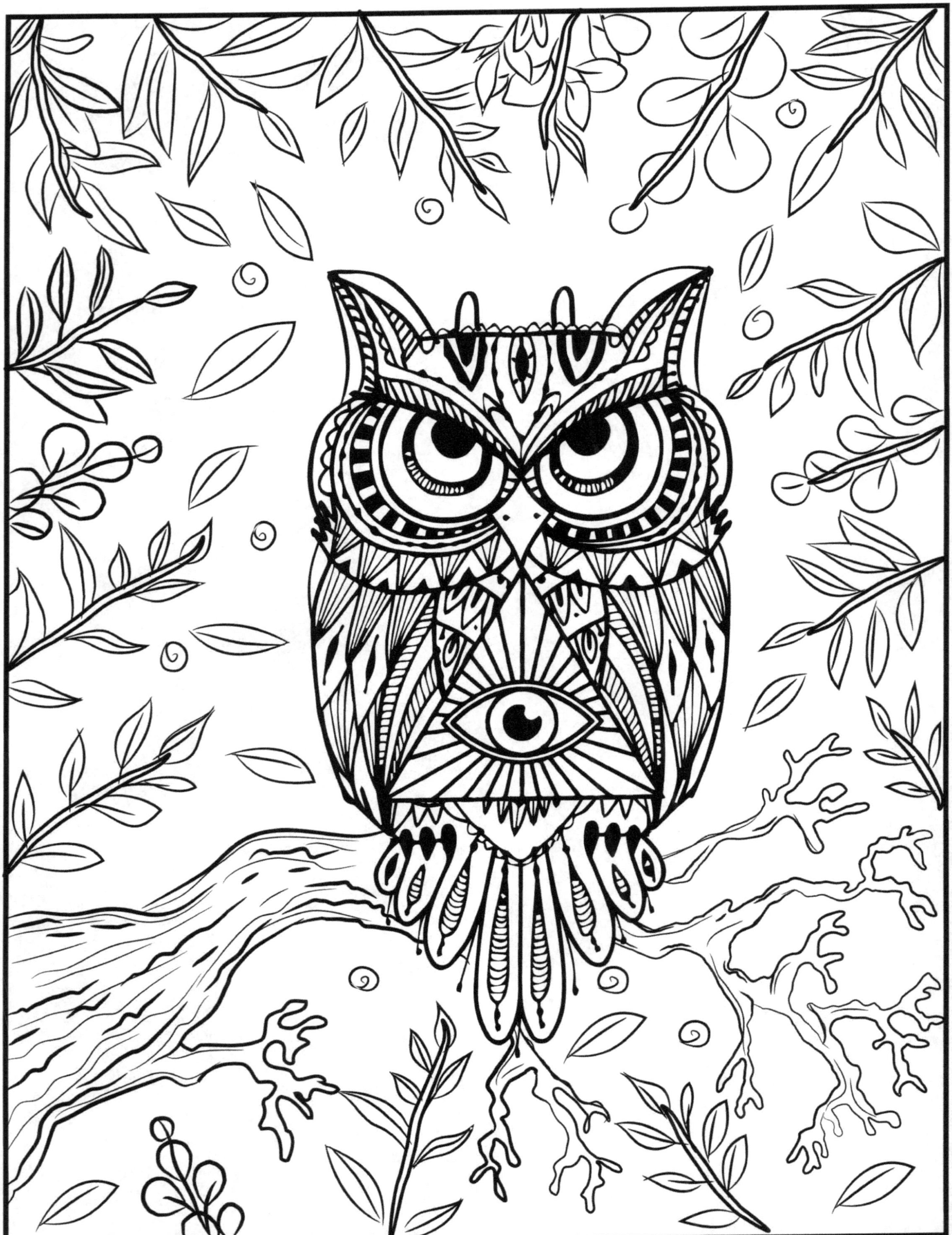

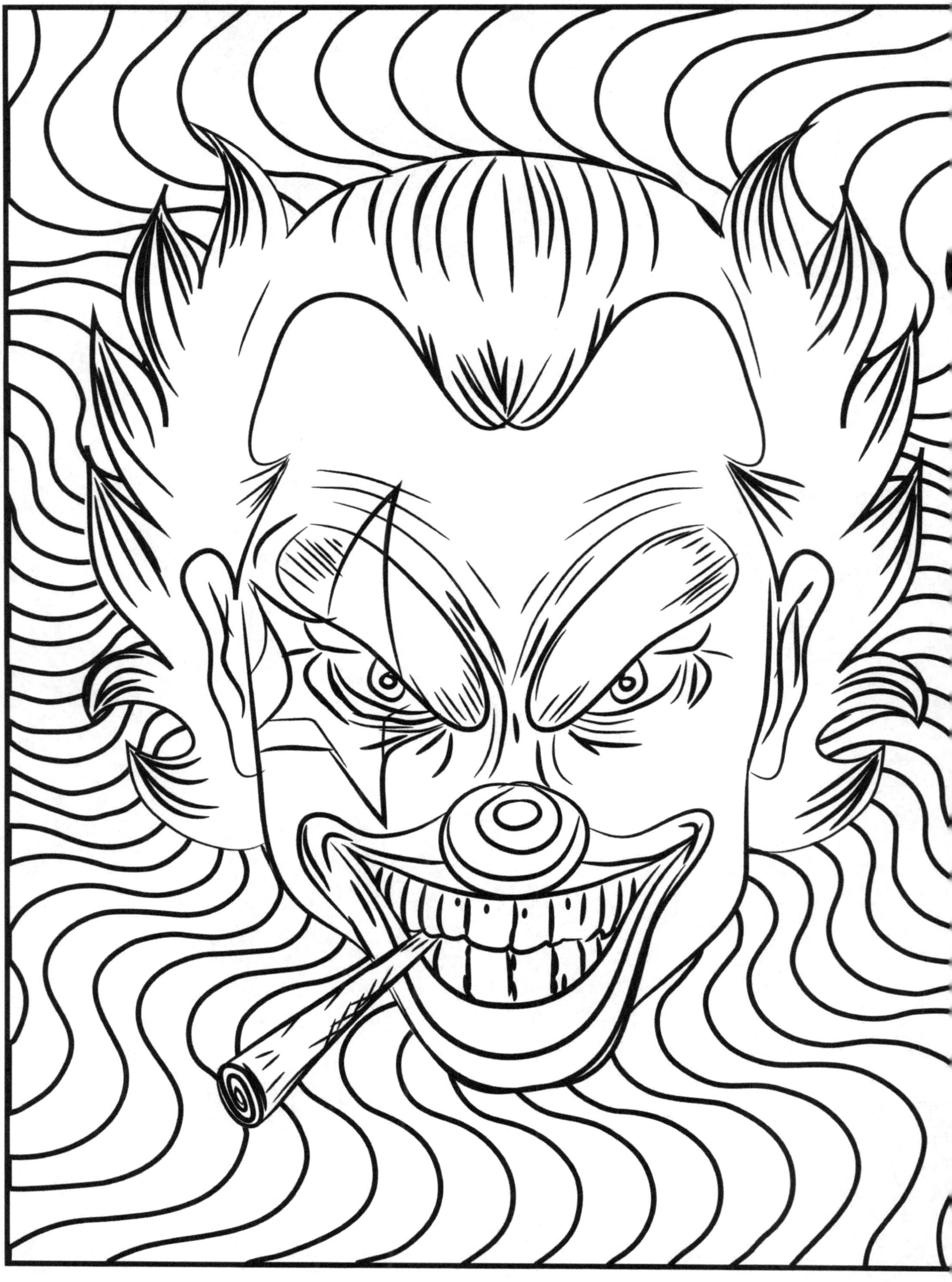

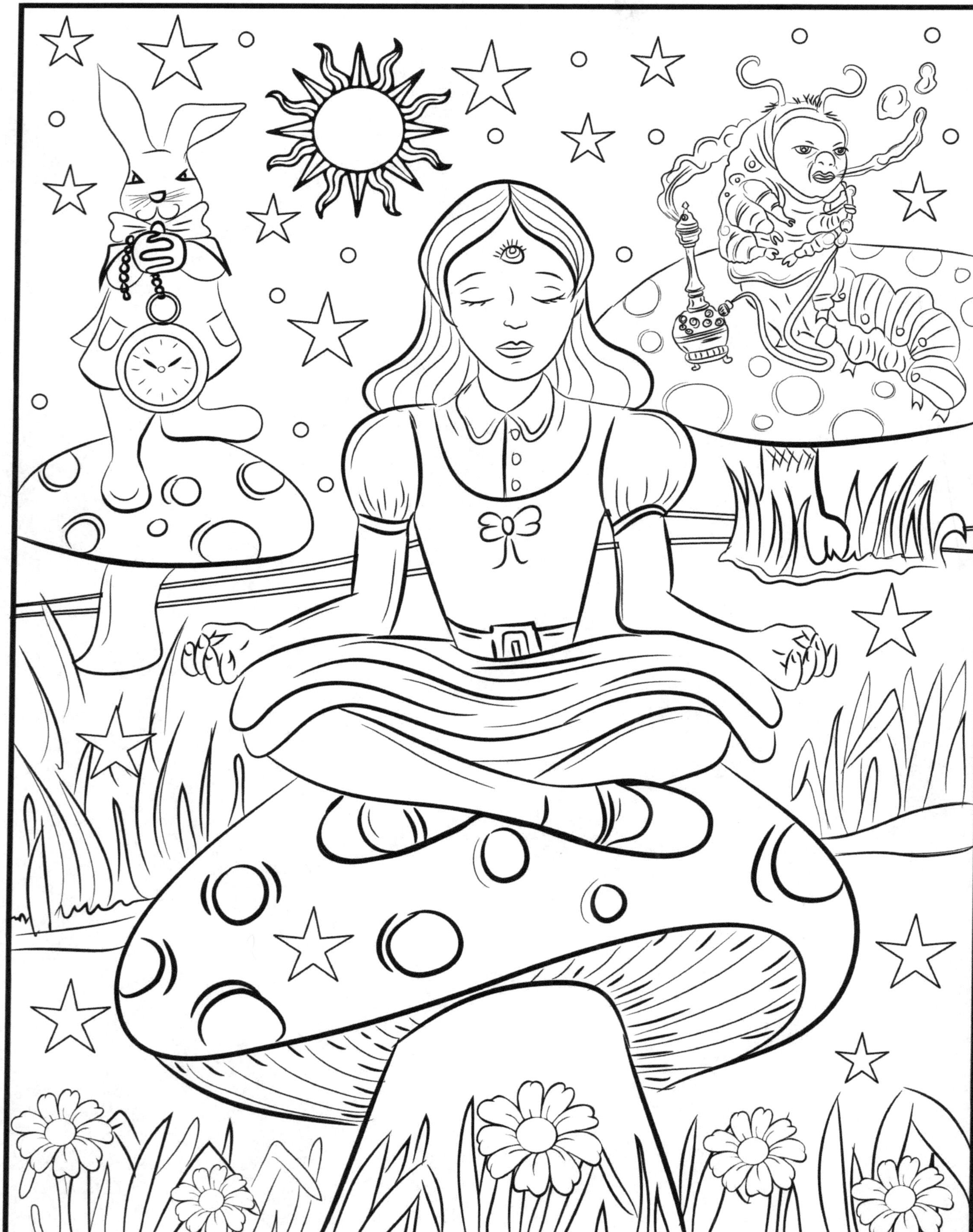

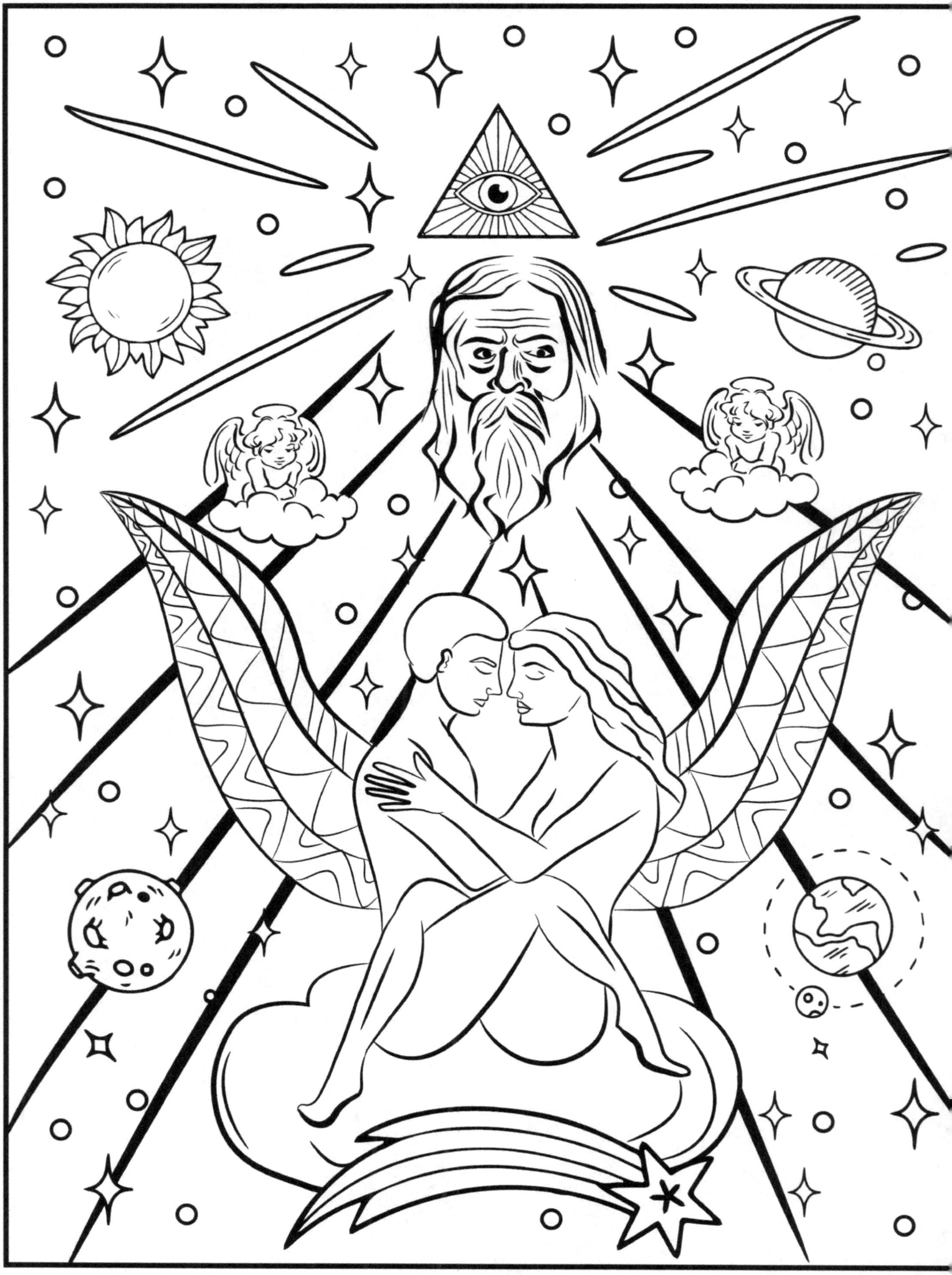

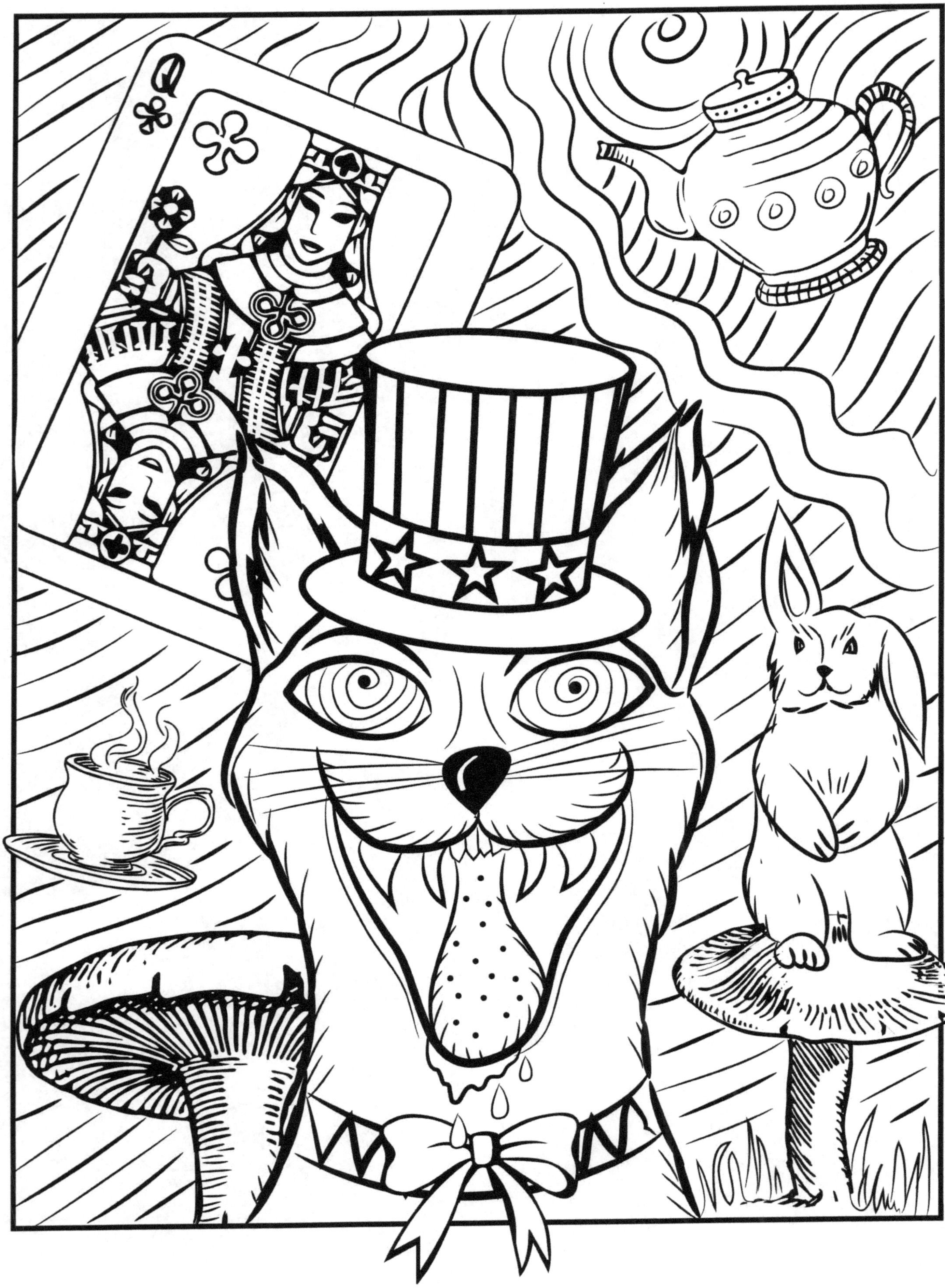

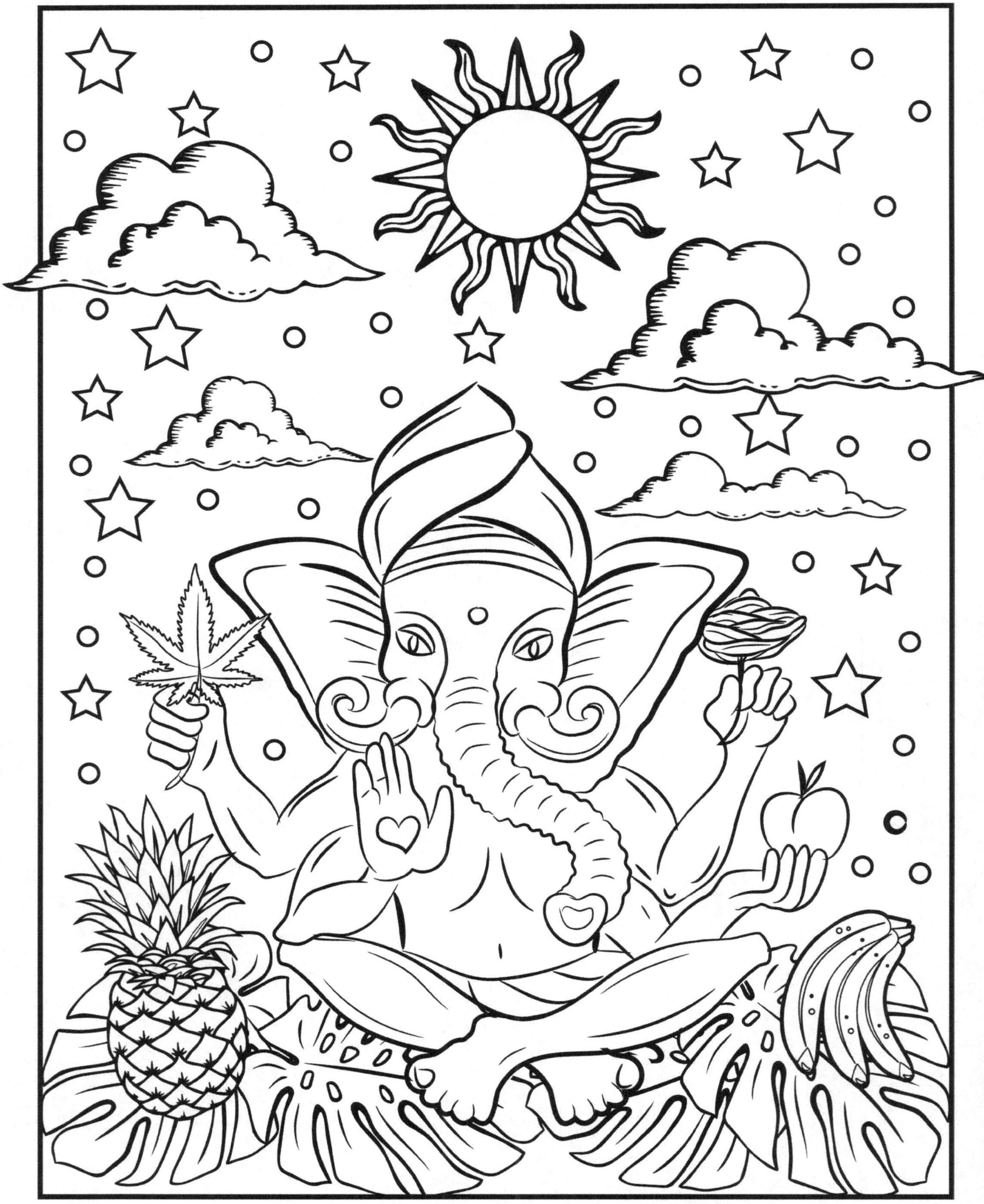

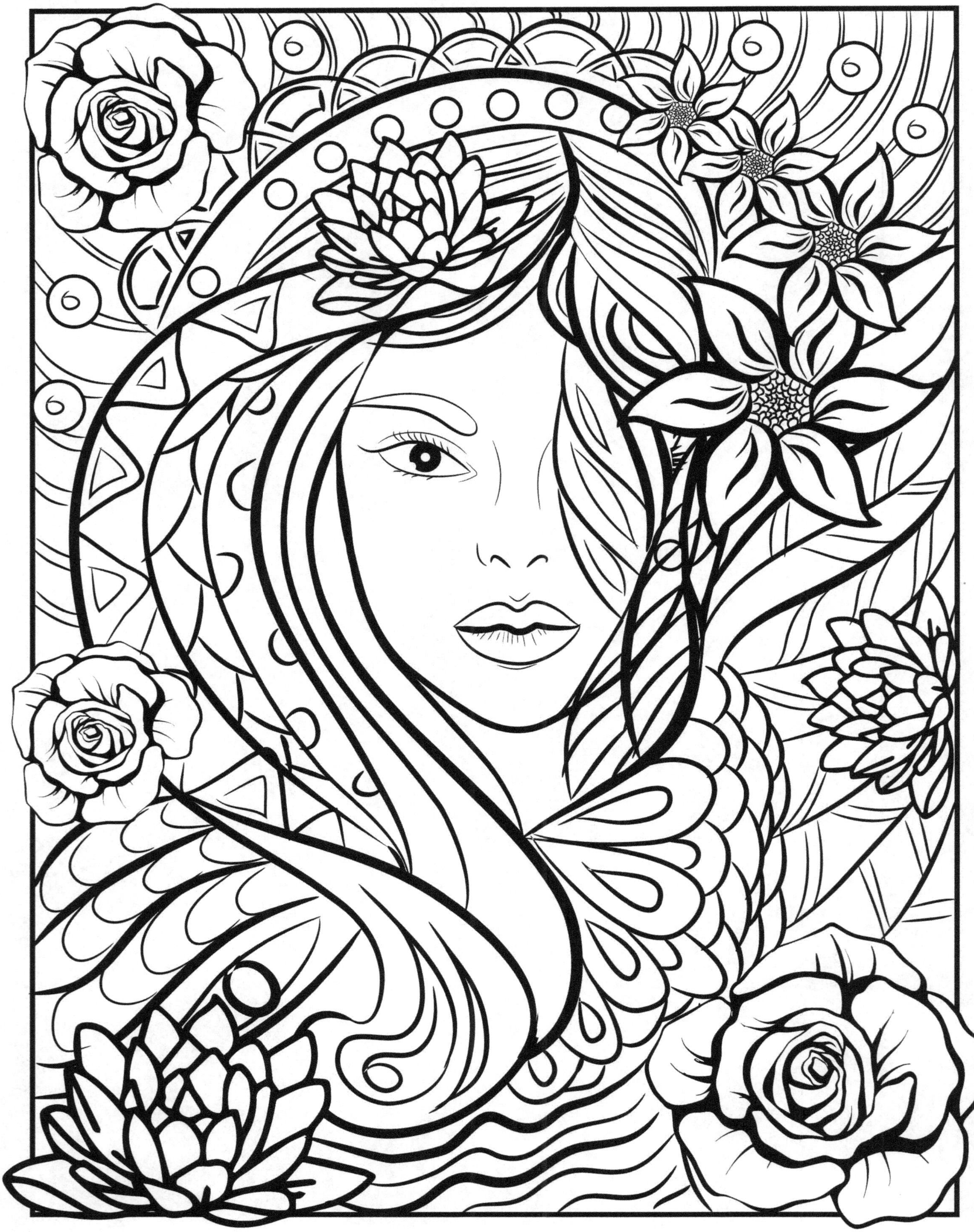

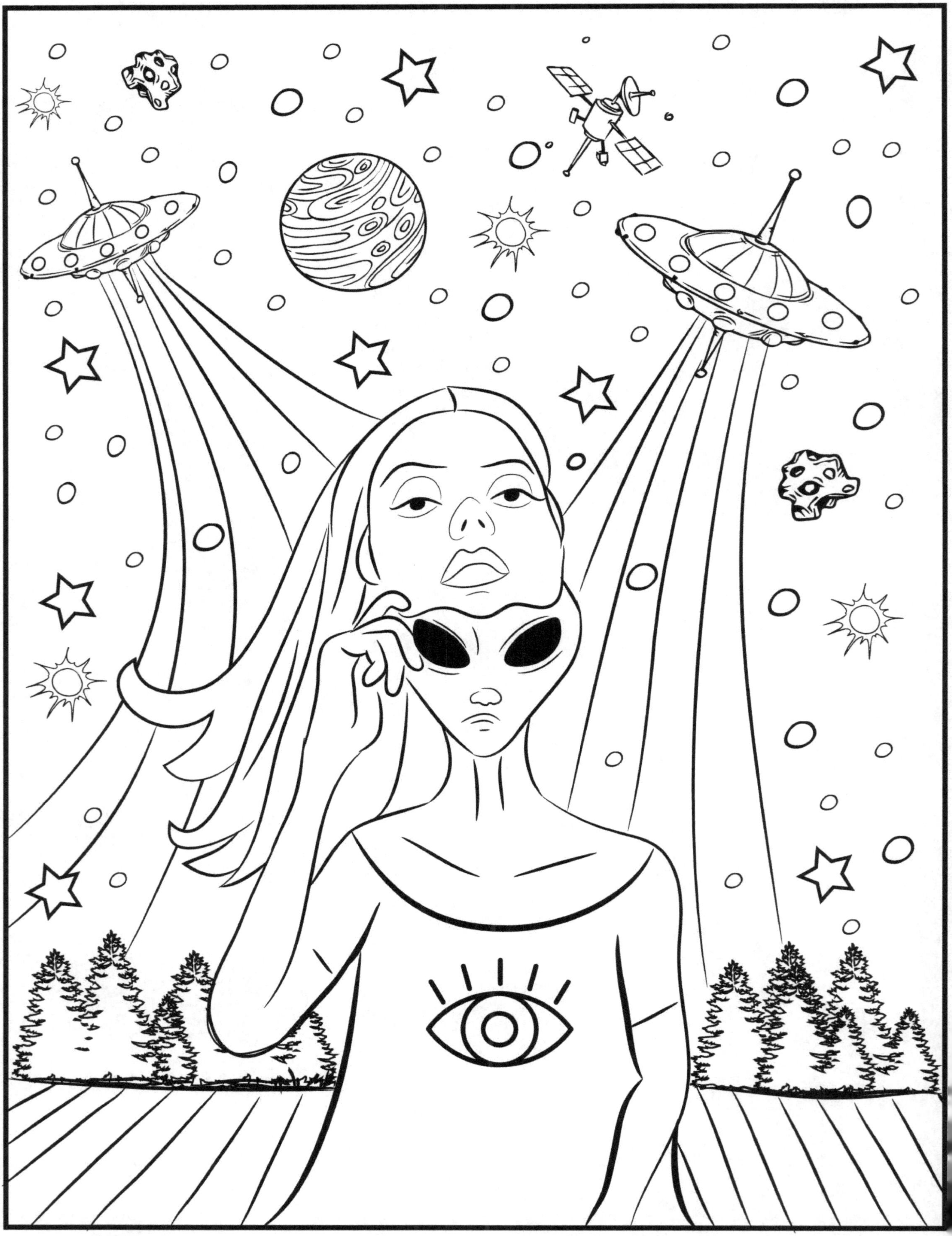

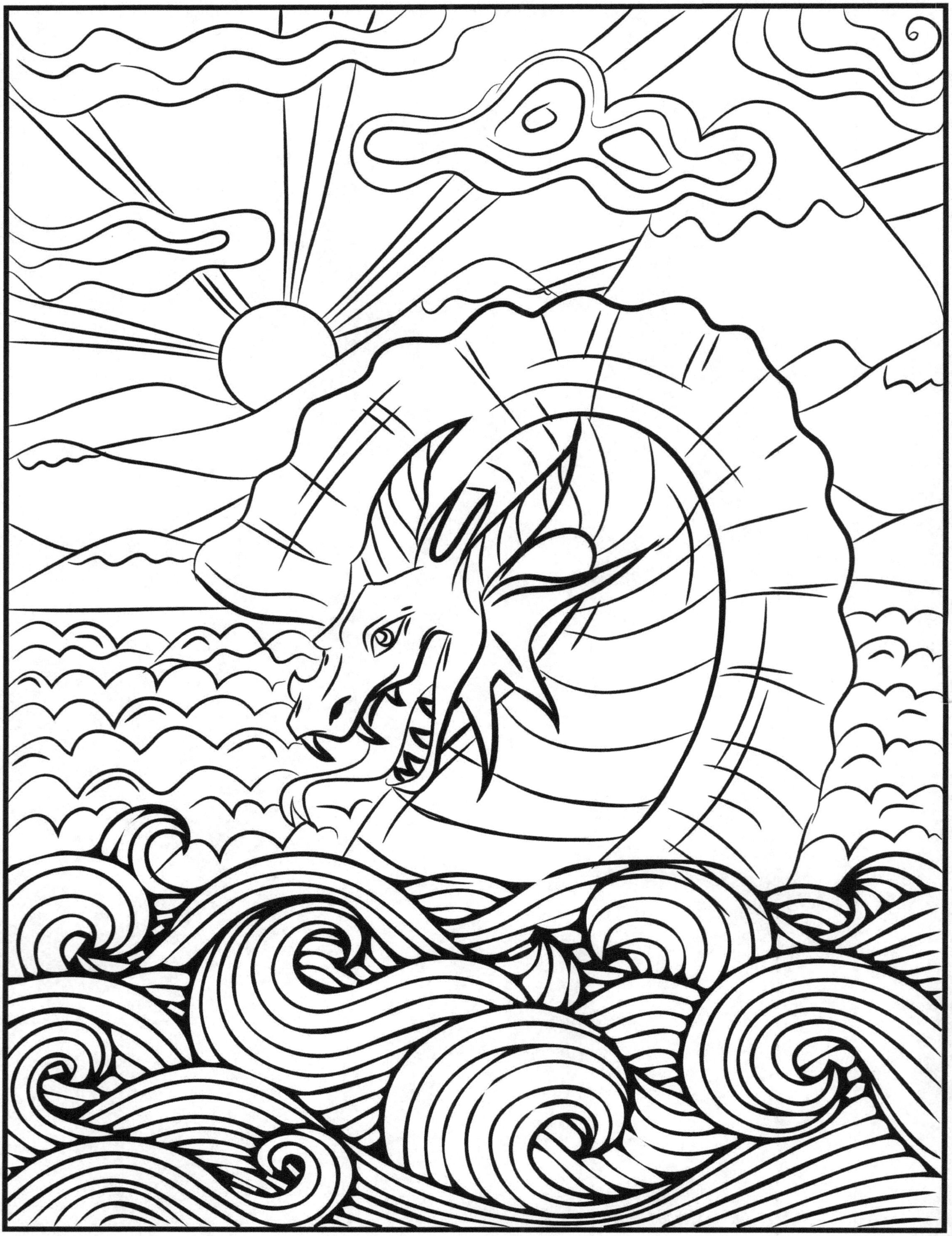

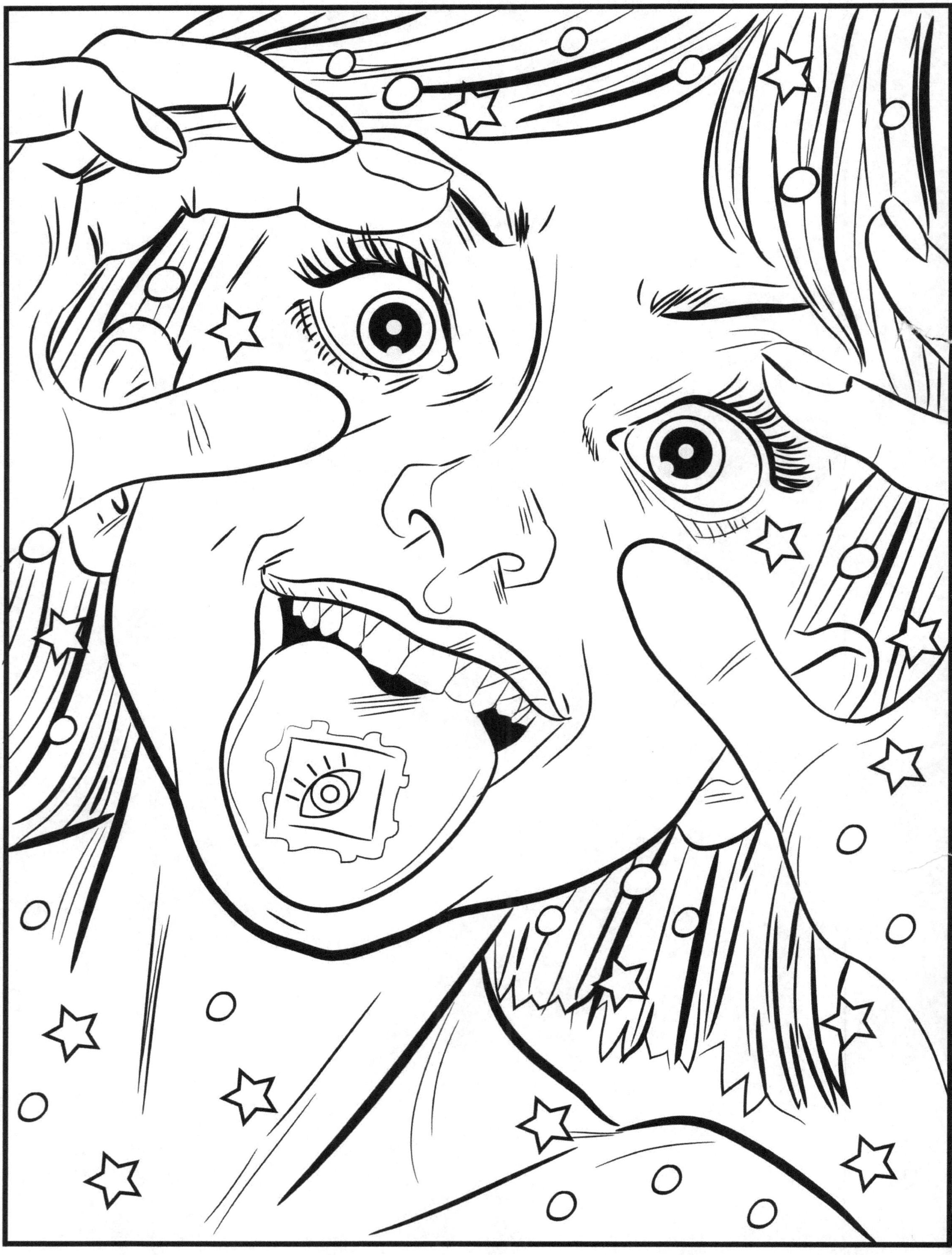

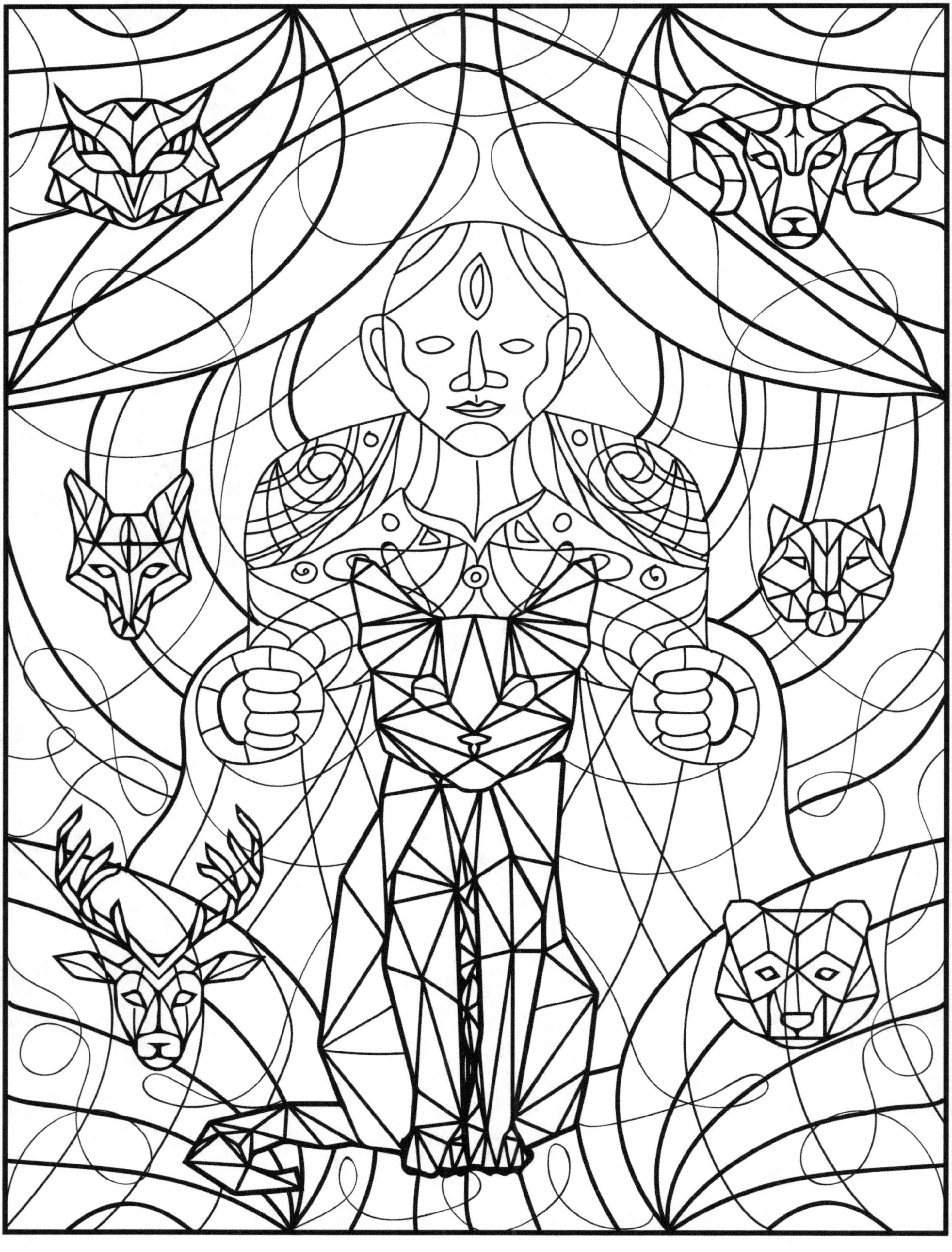

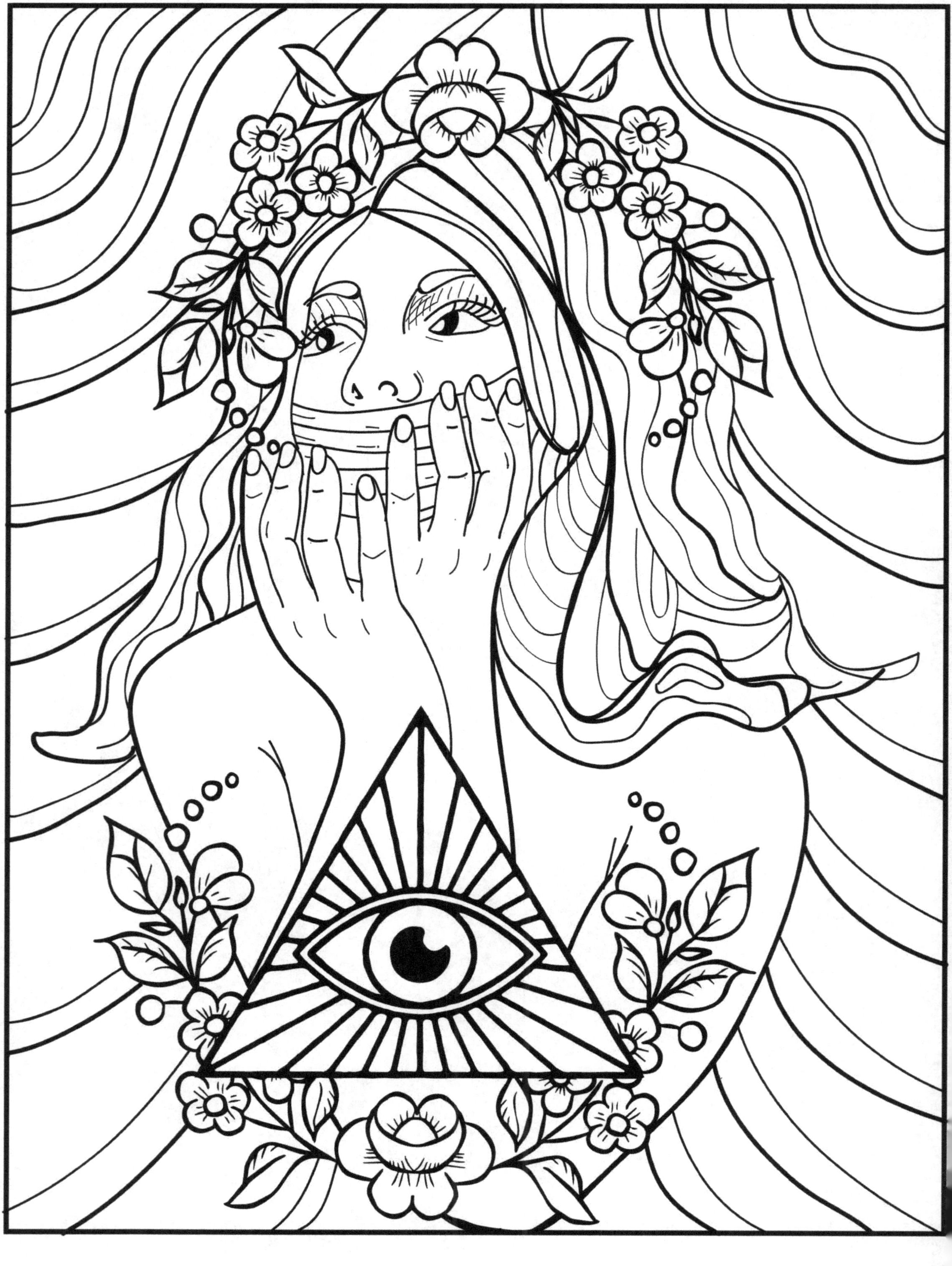

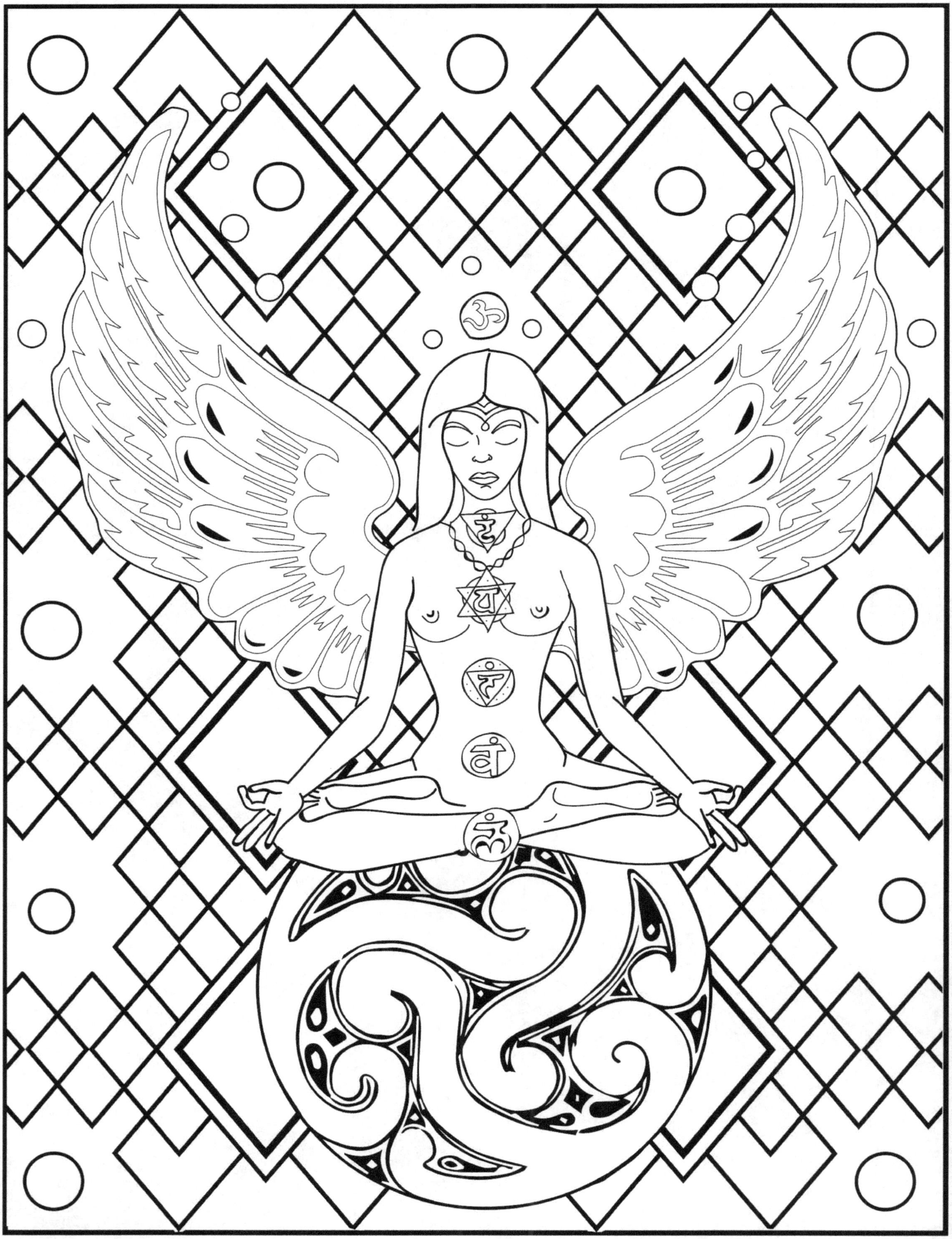

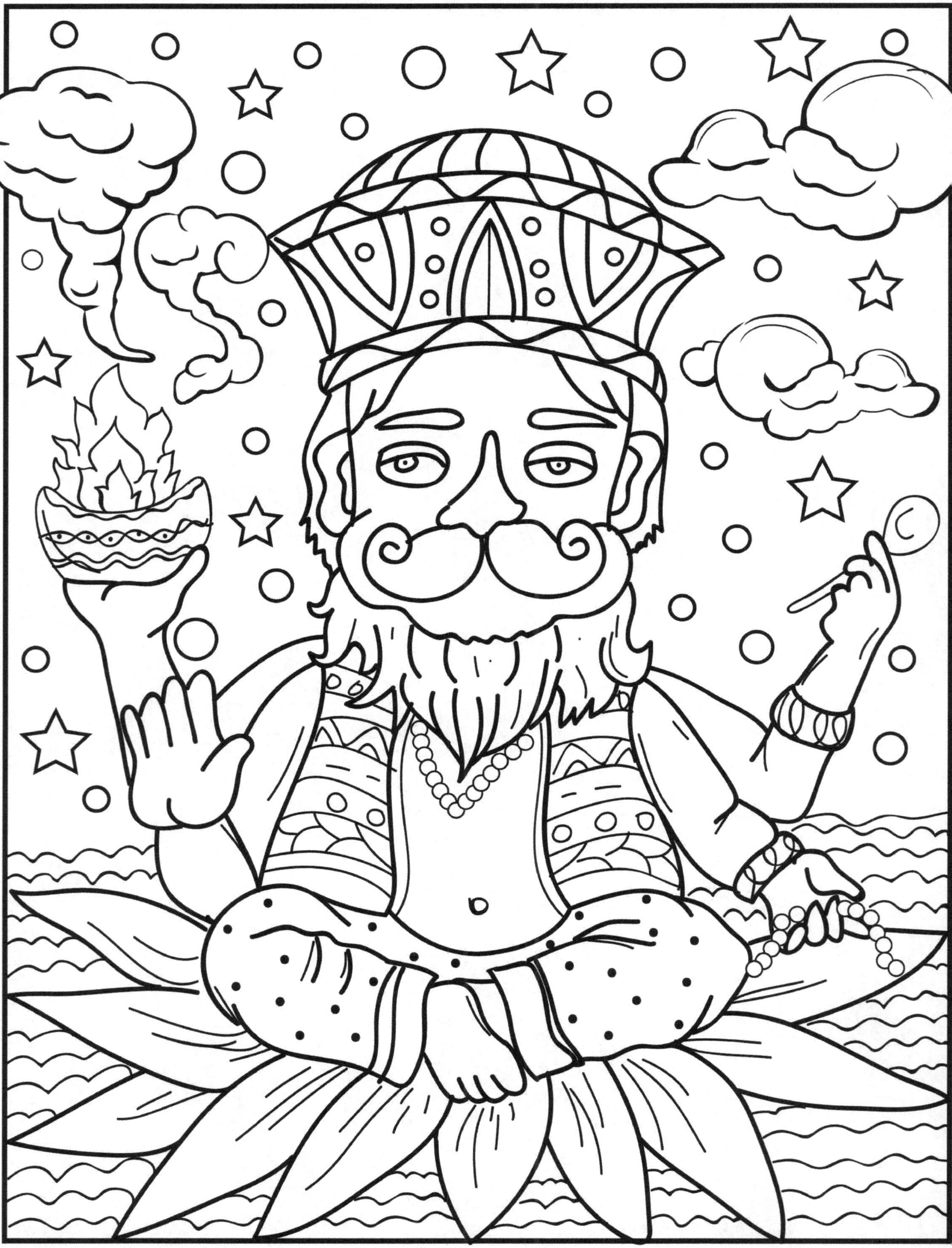

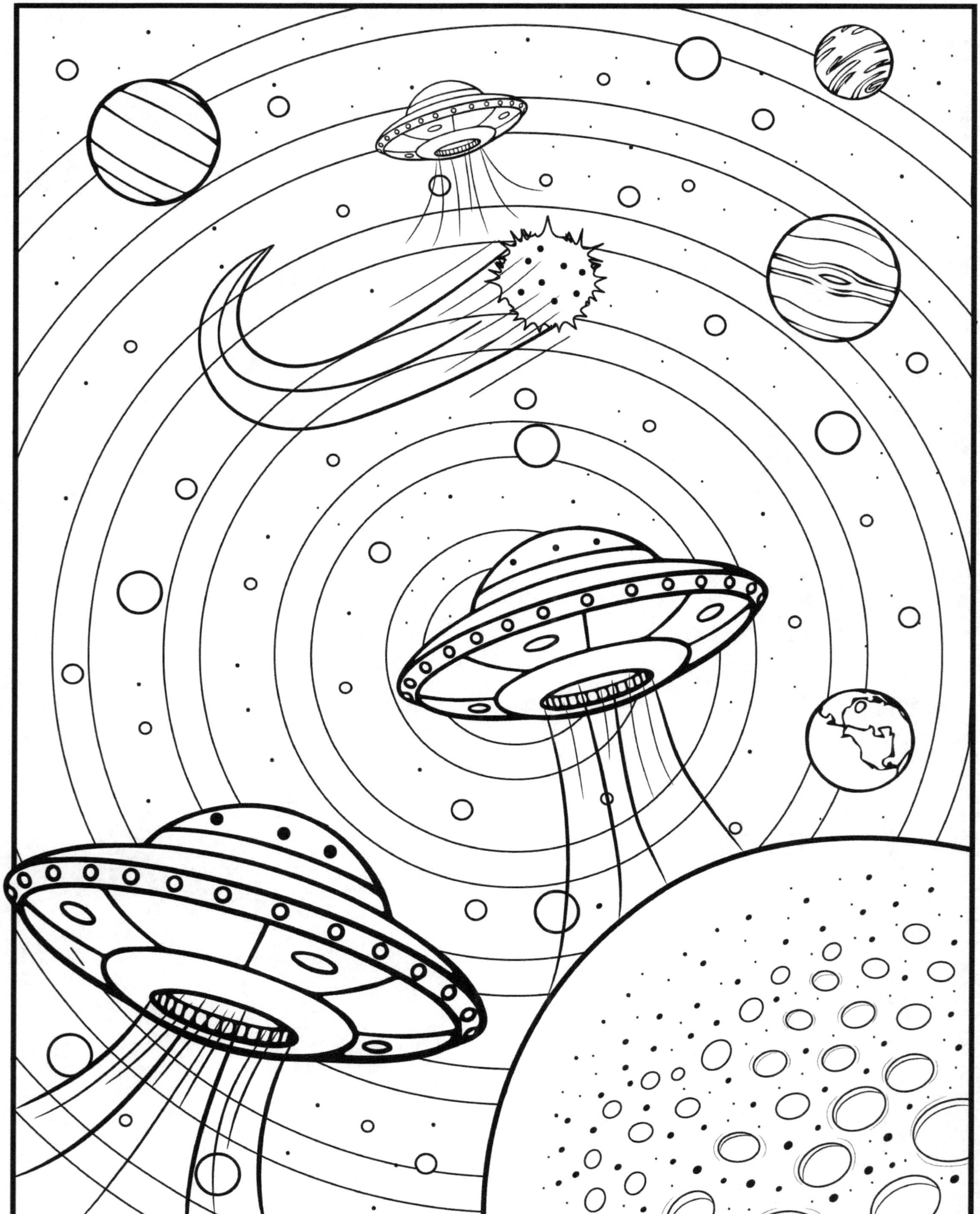

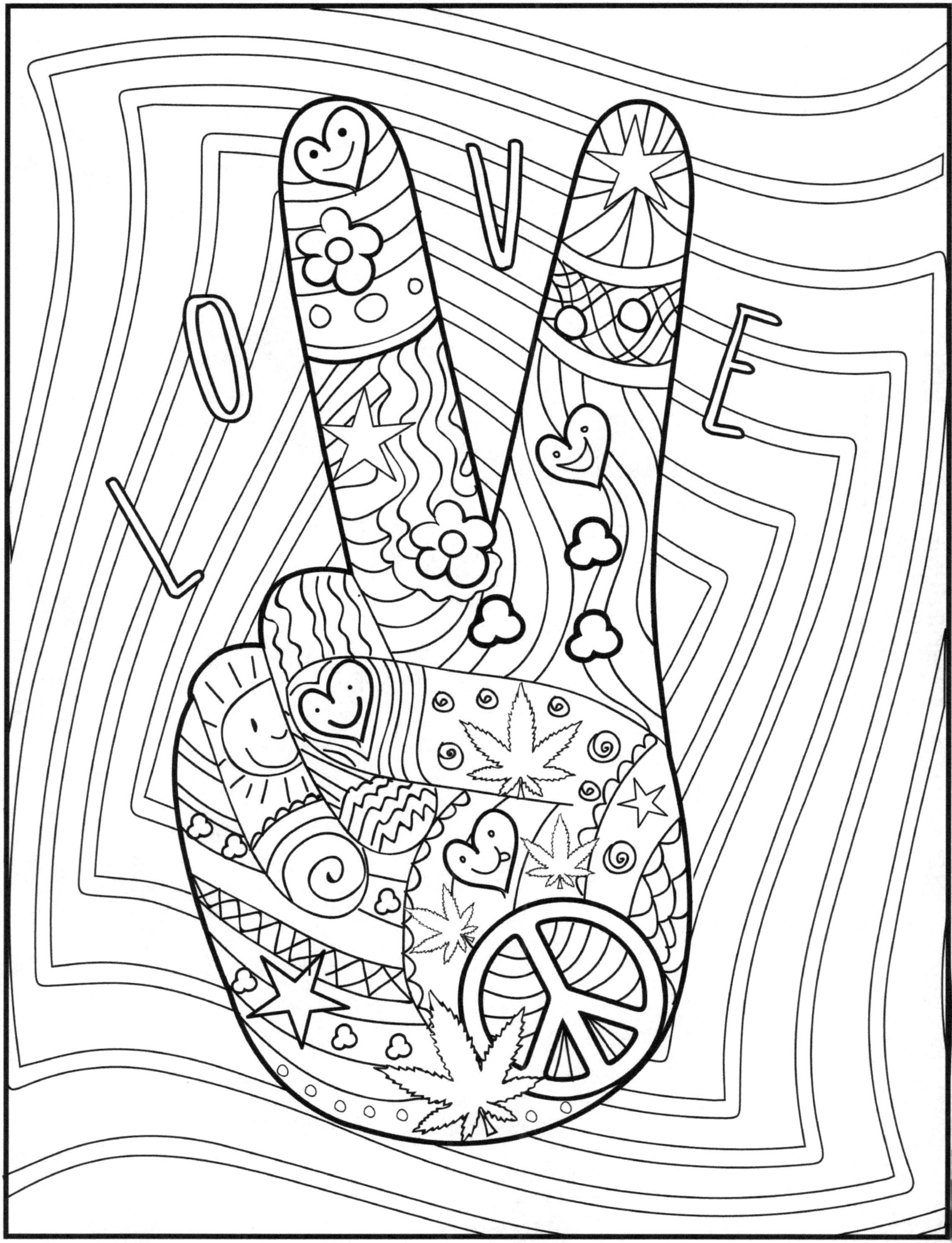
LOVE

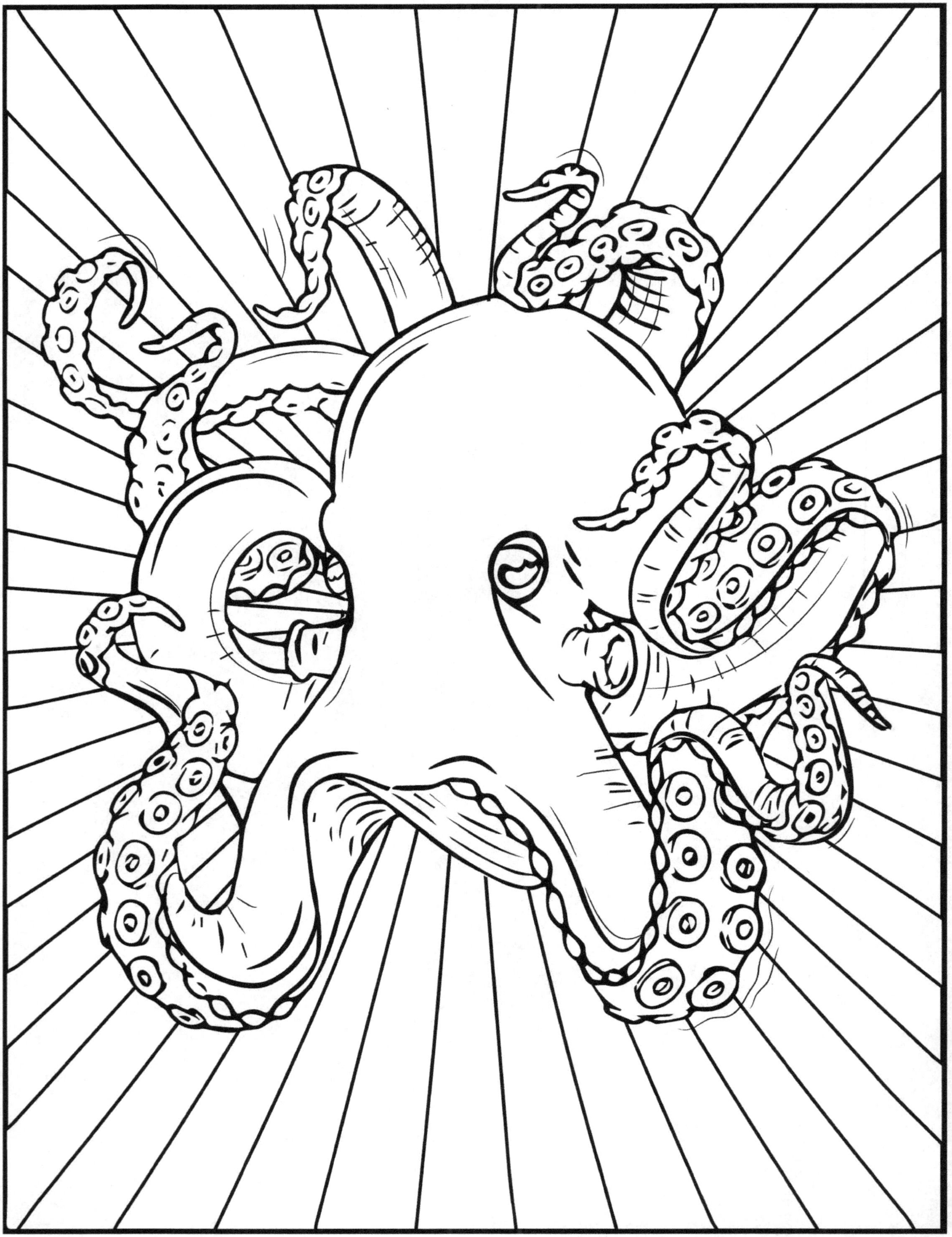

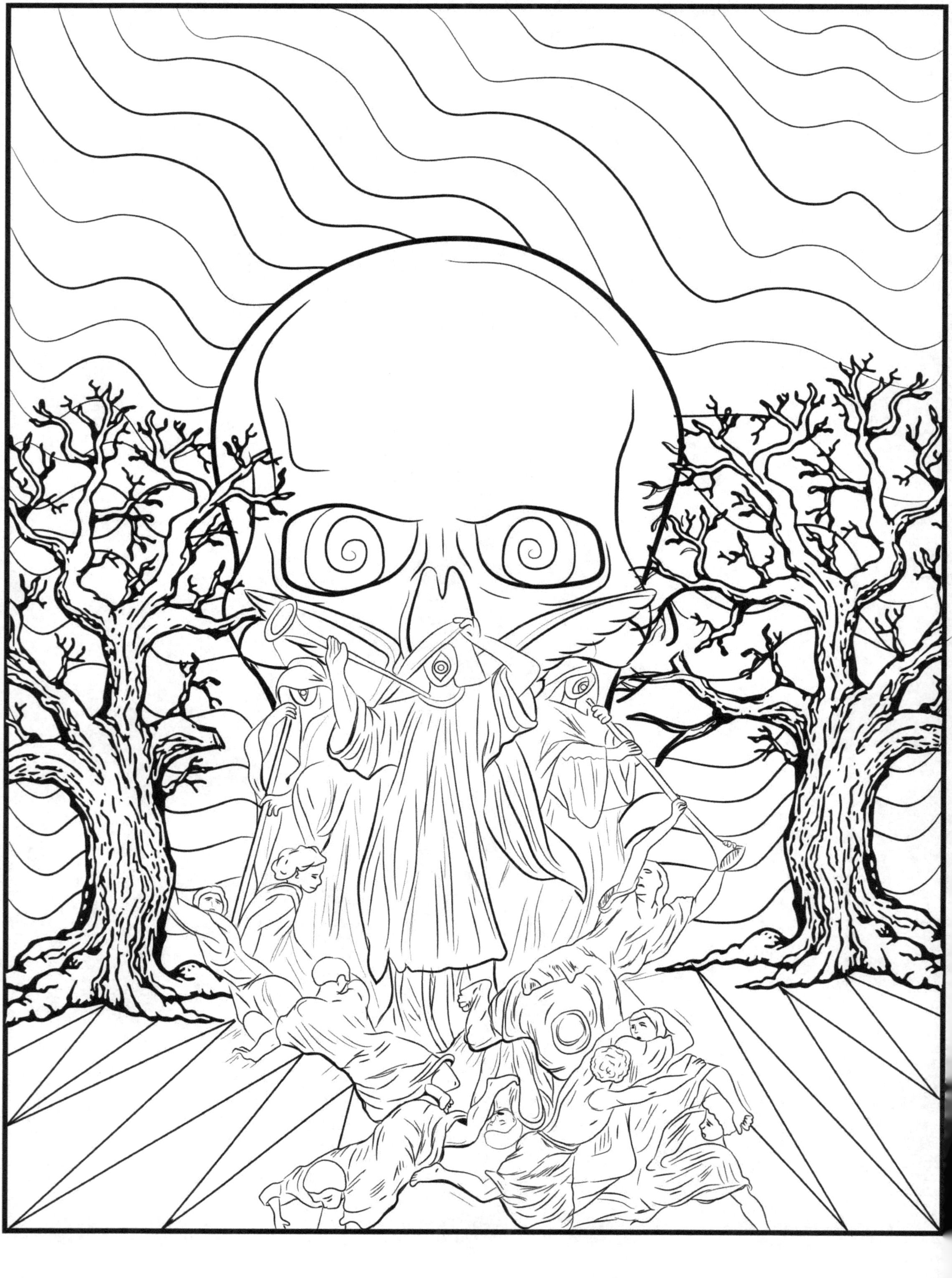

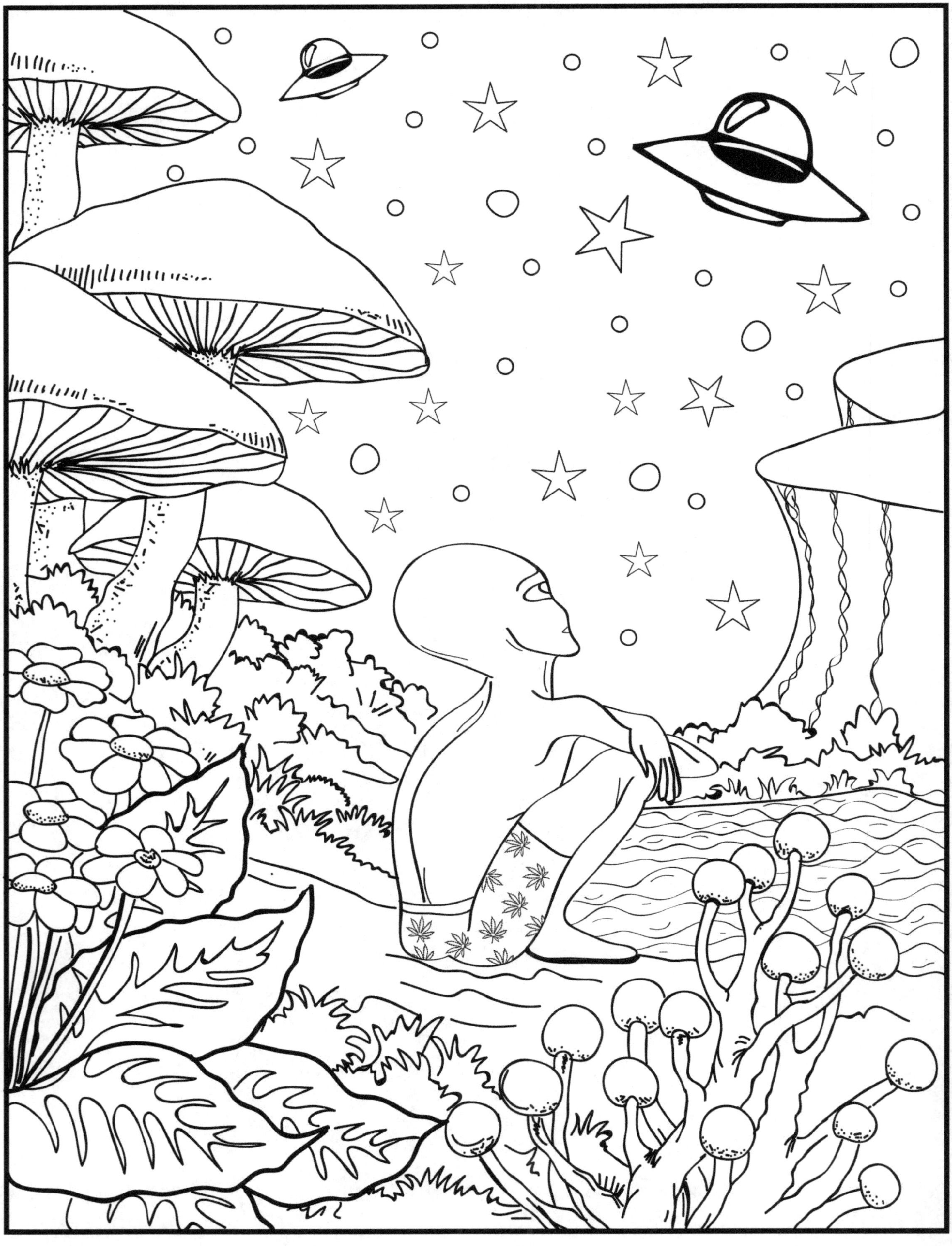

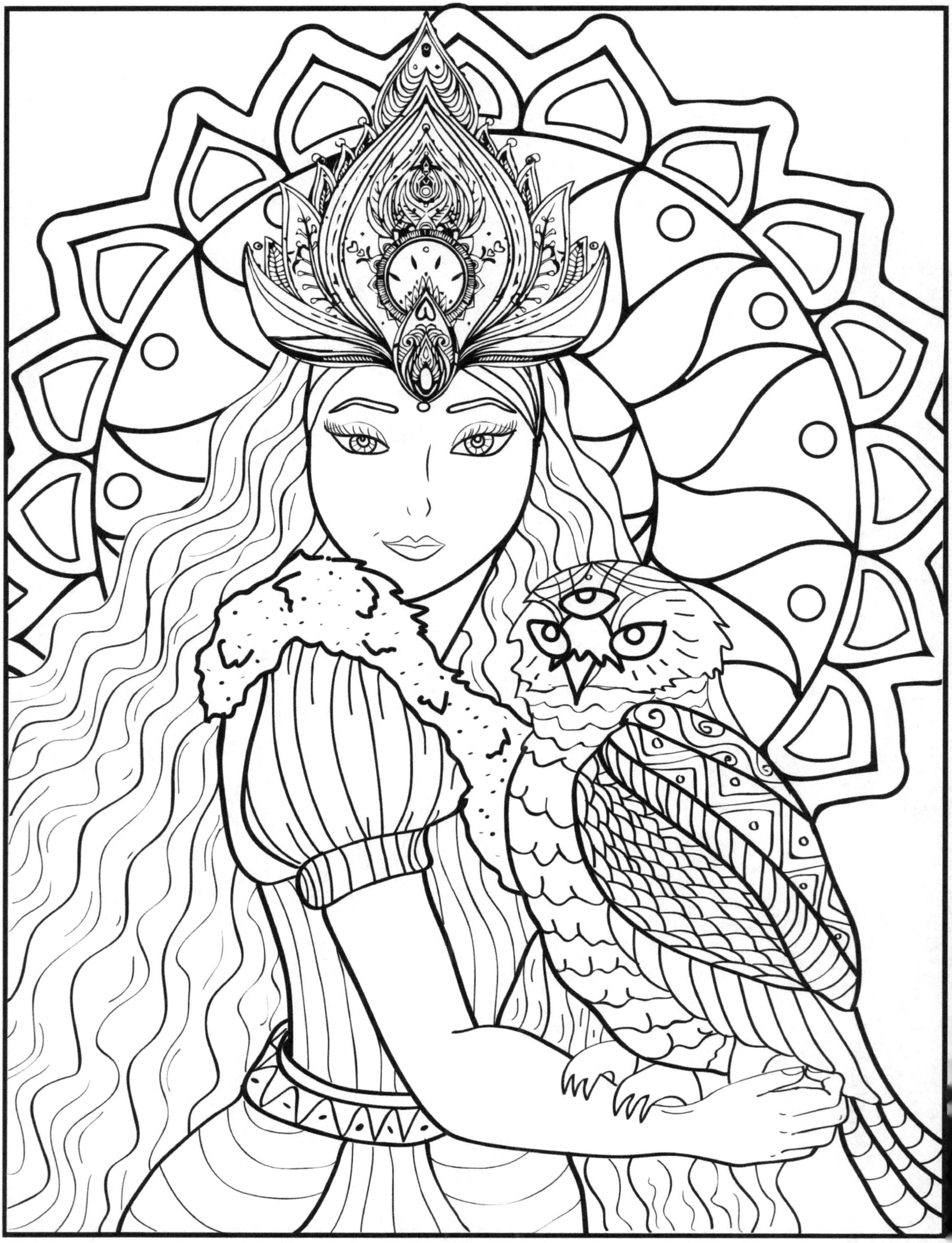

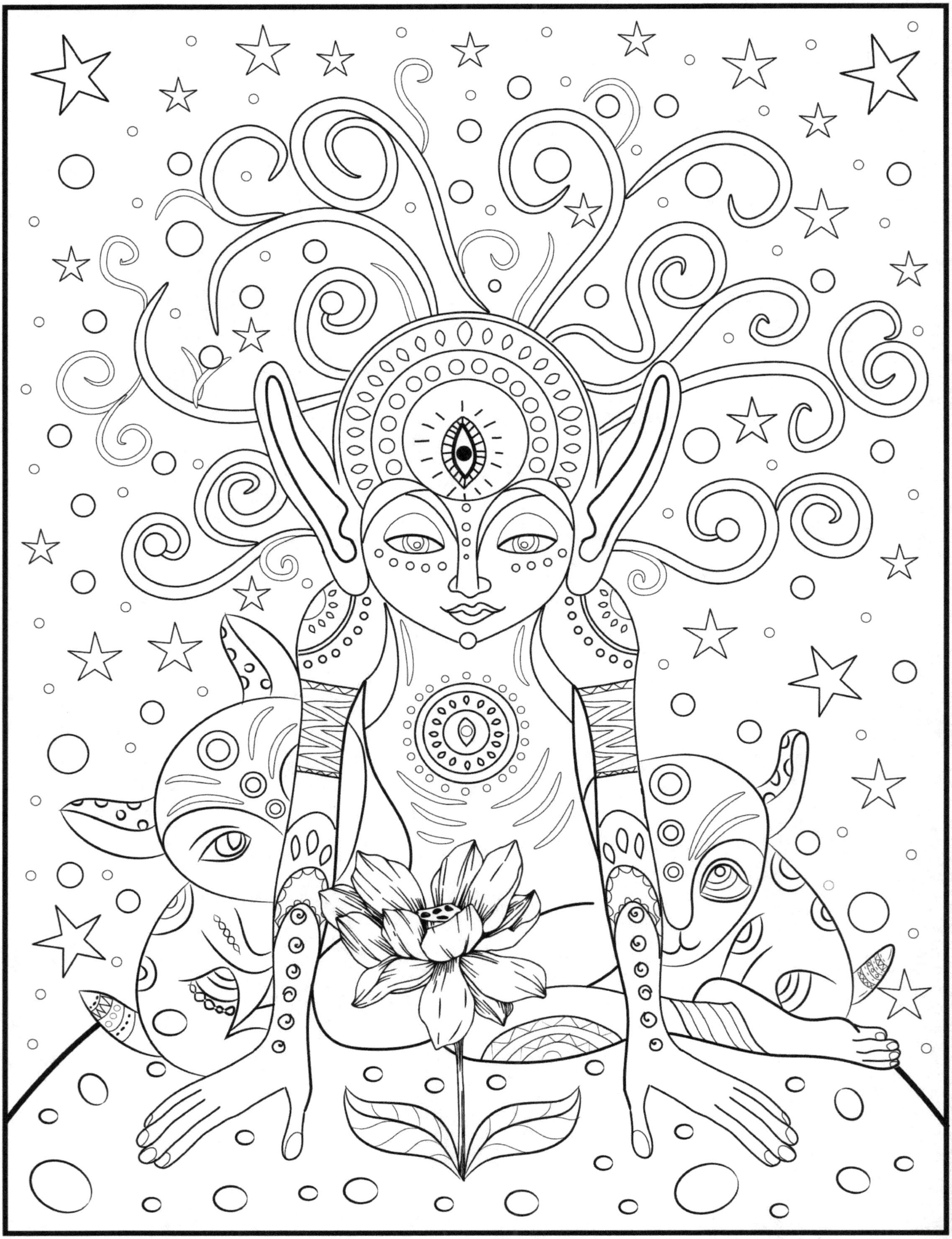

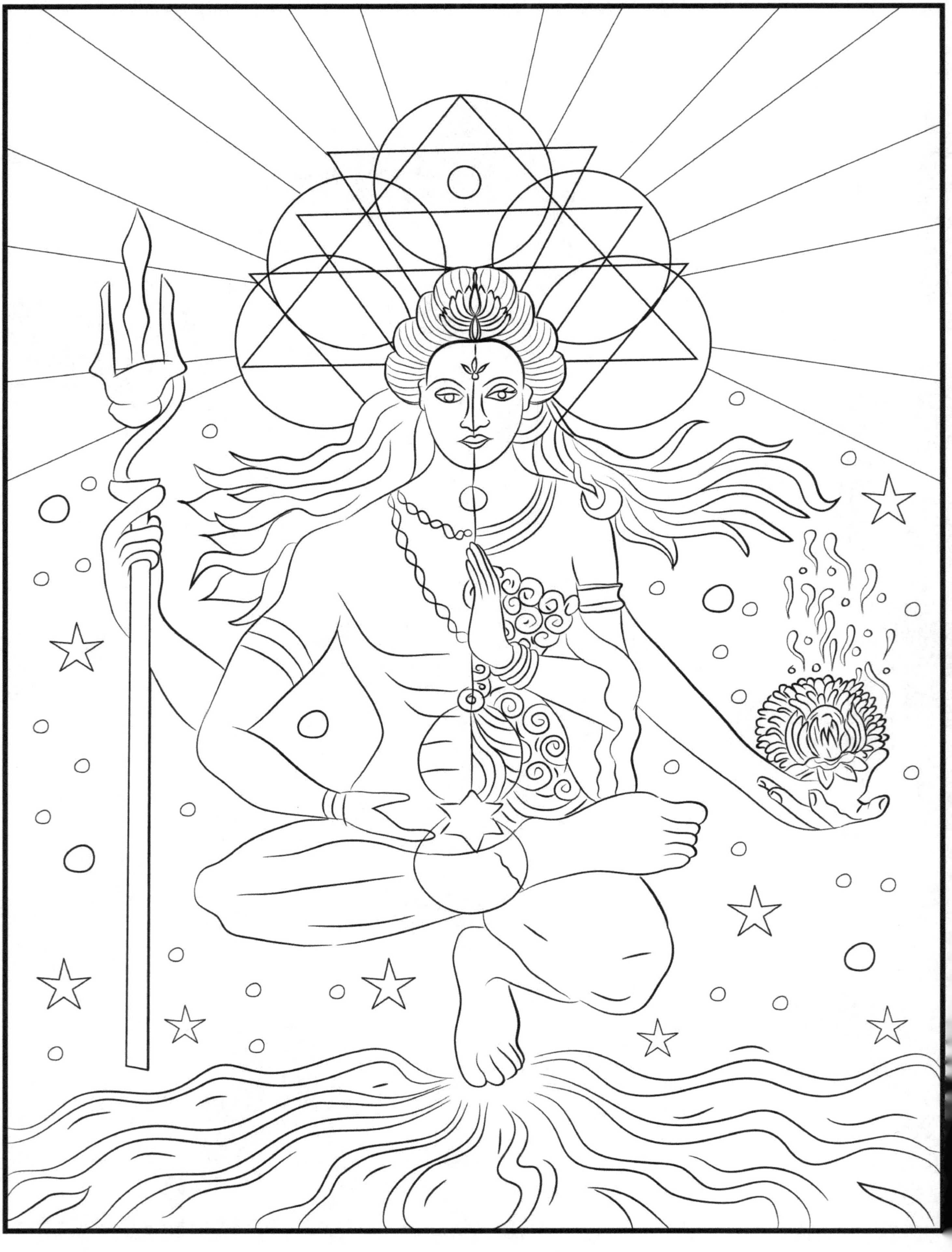

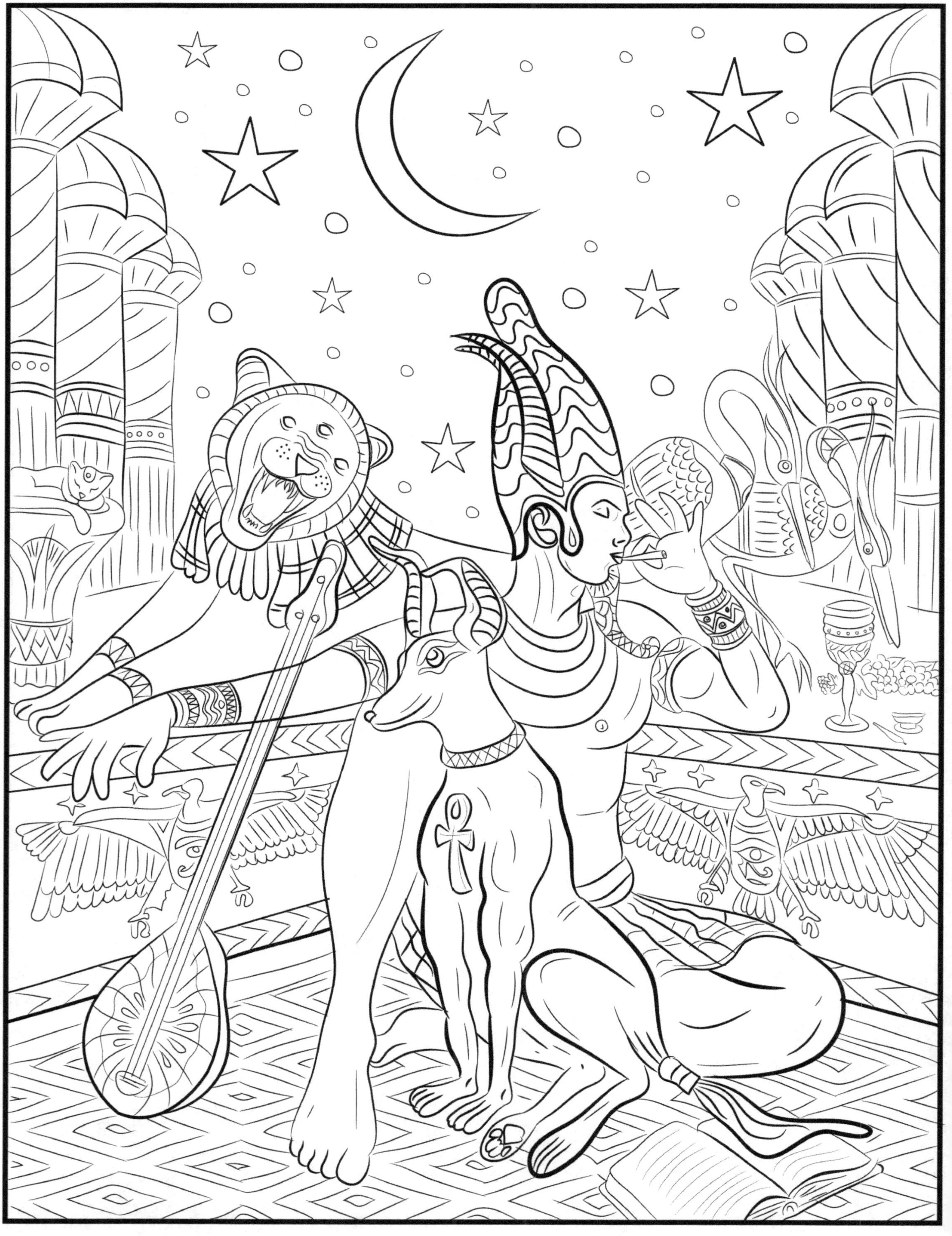

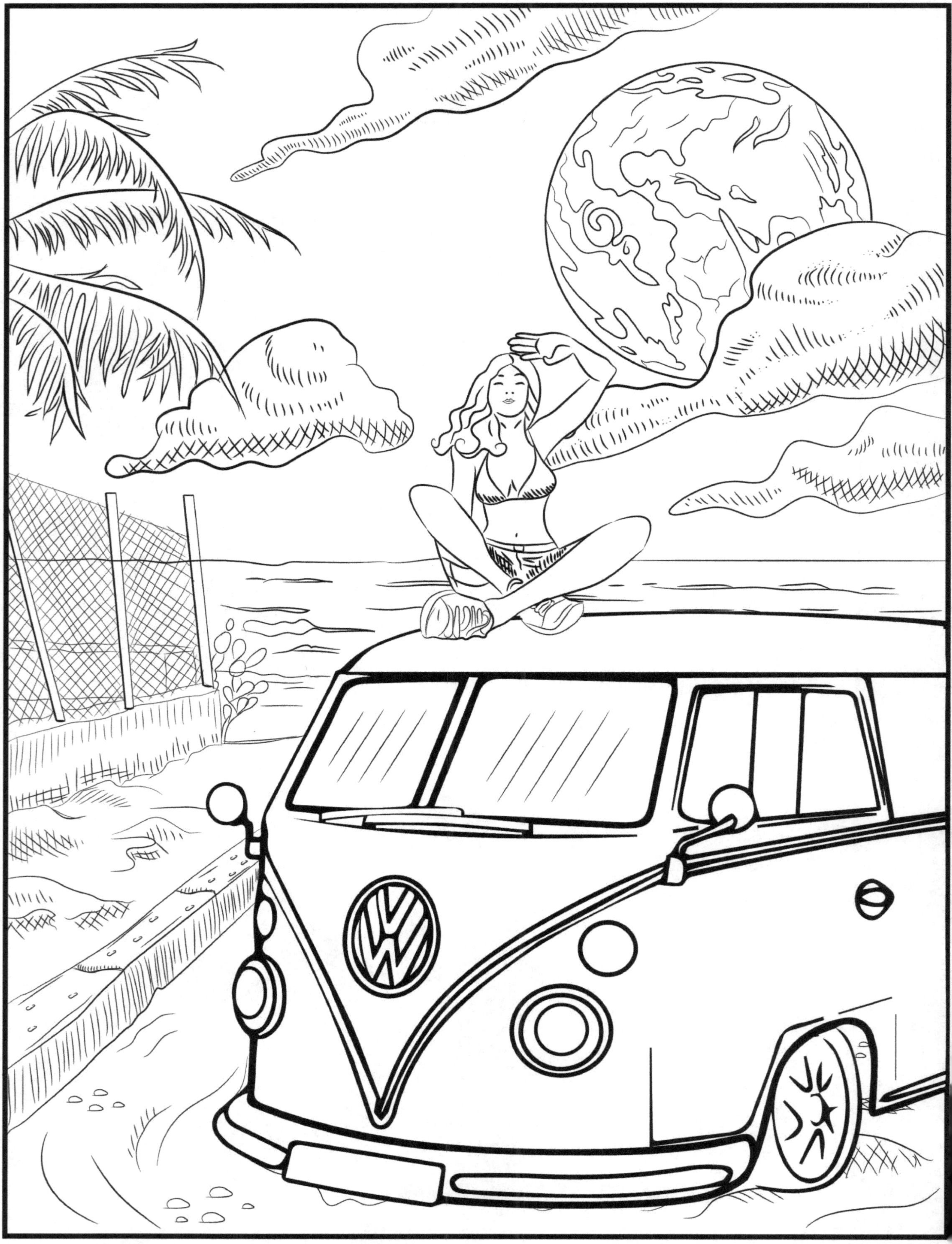

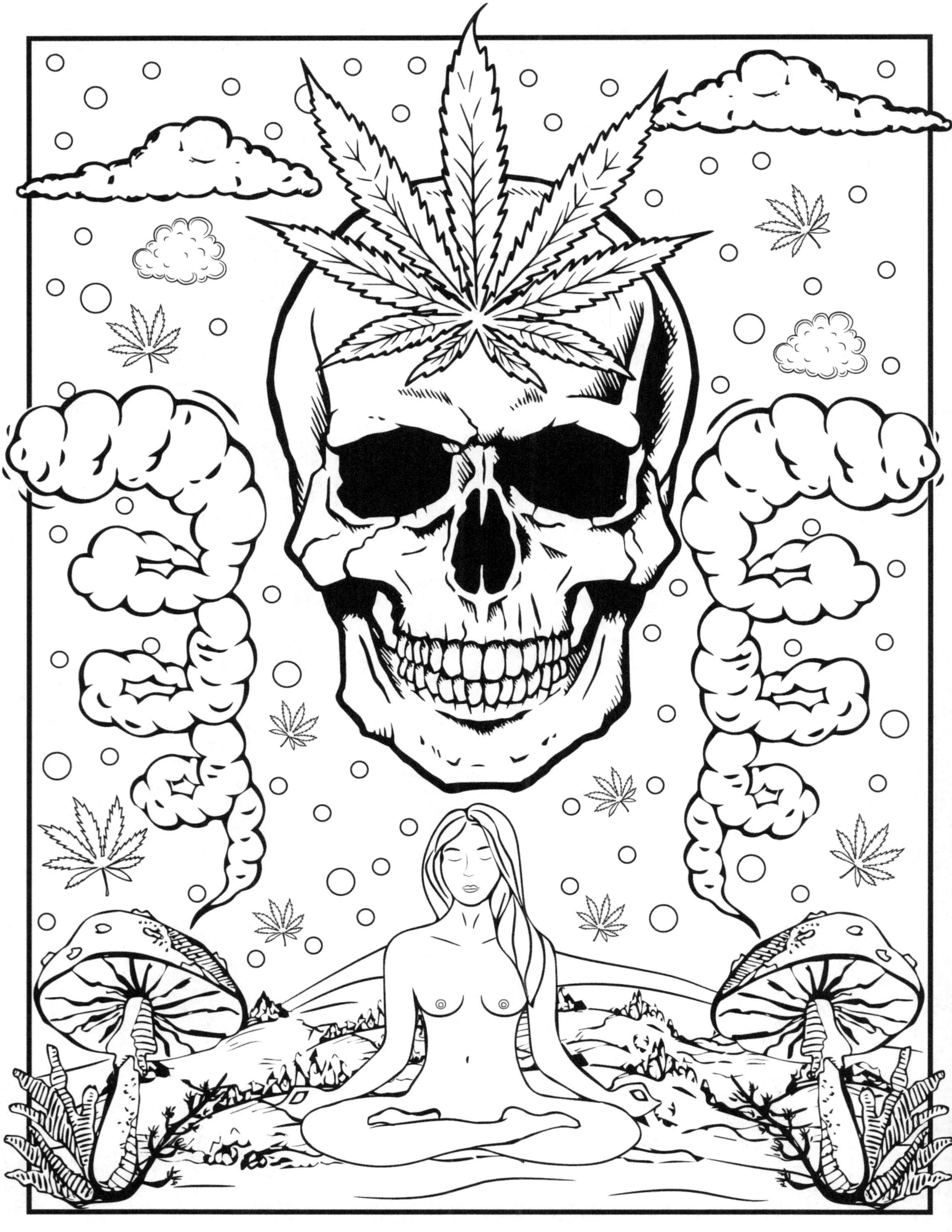

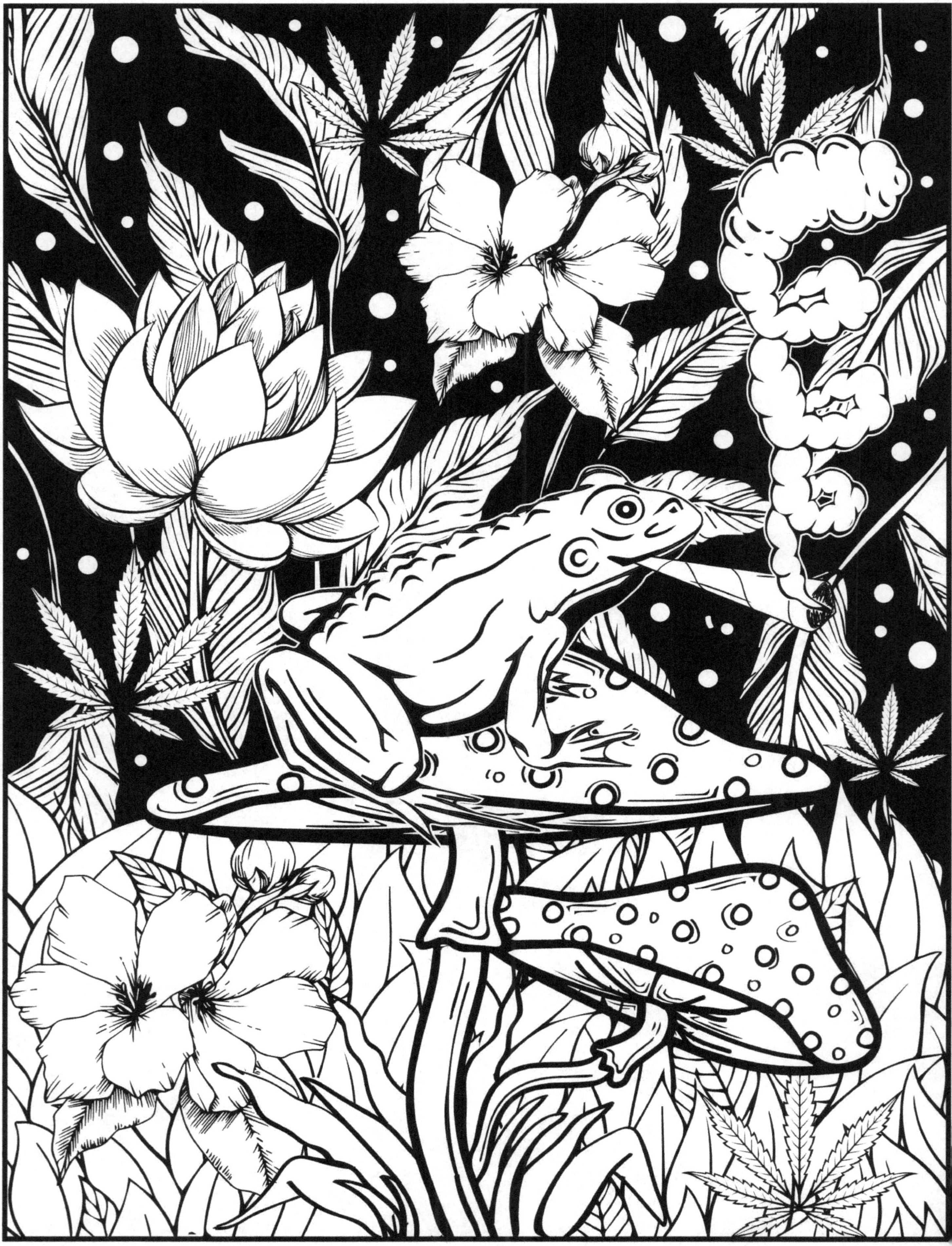

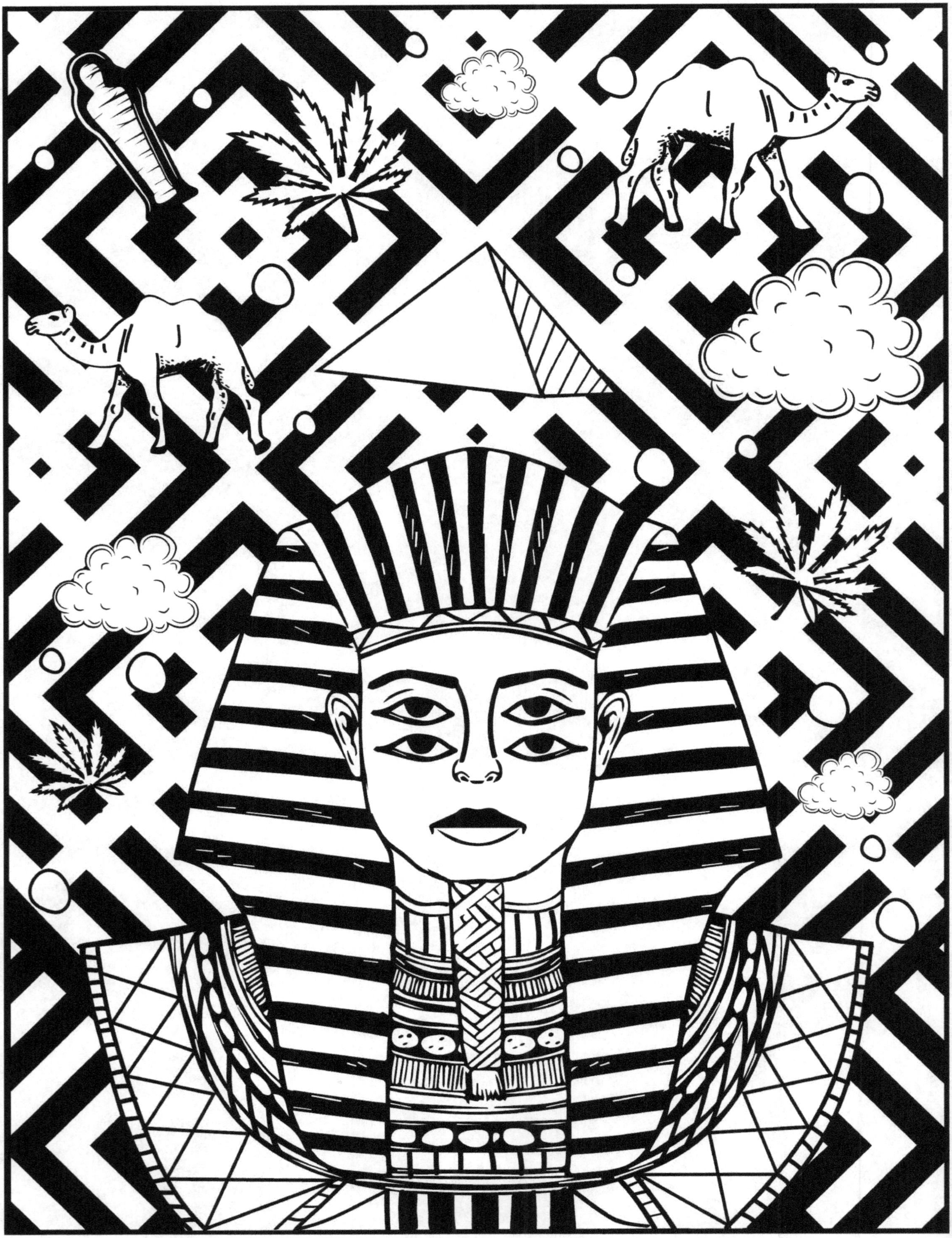

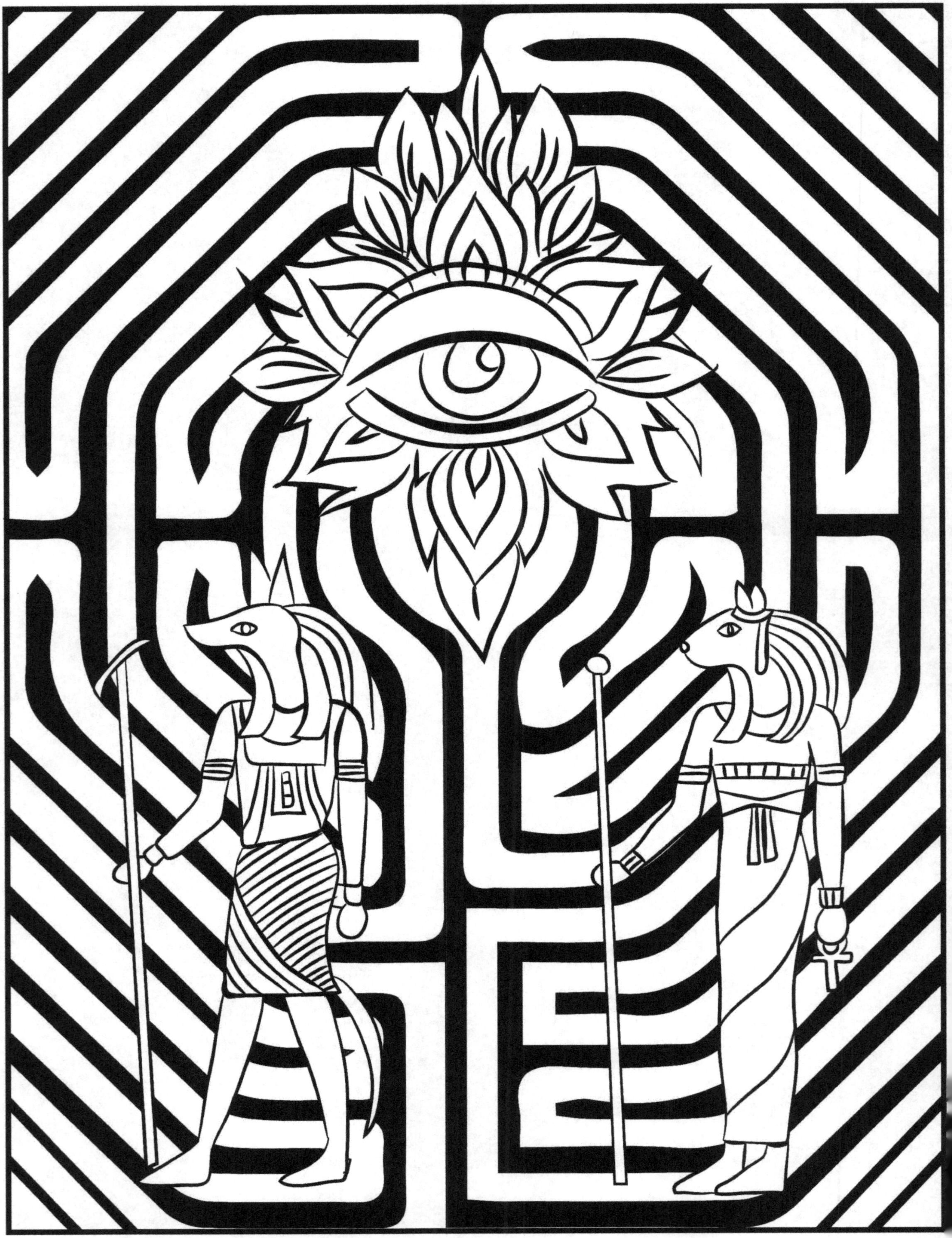

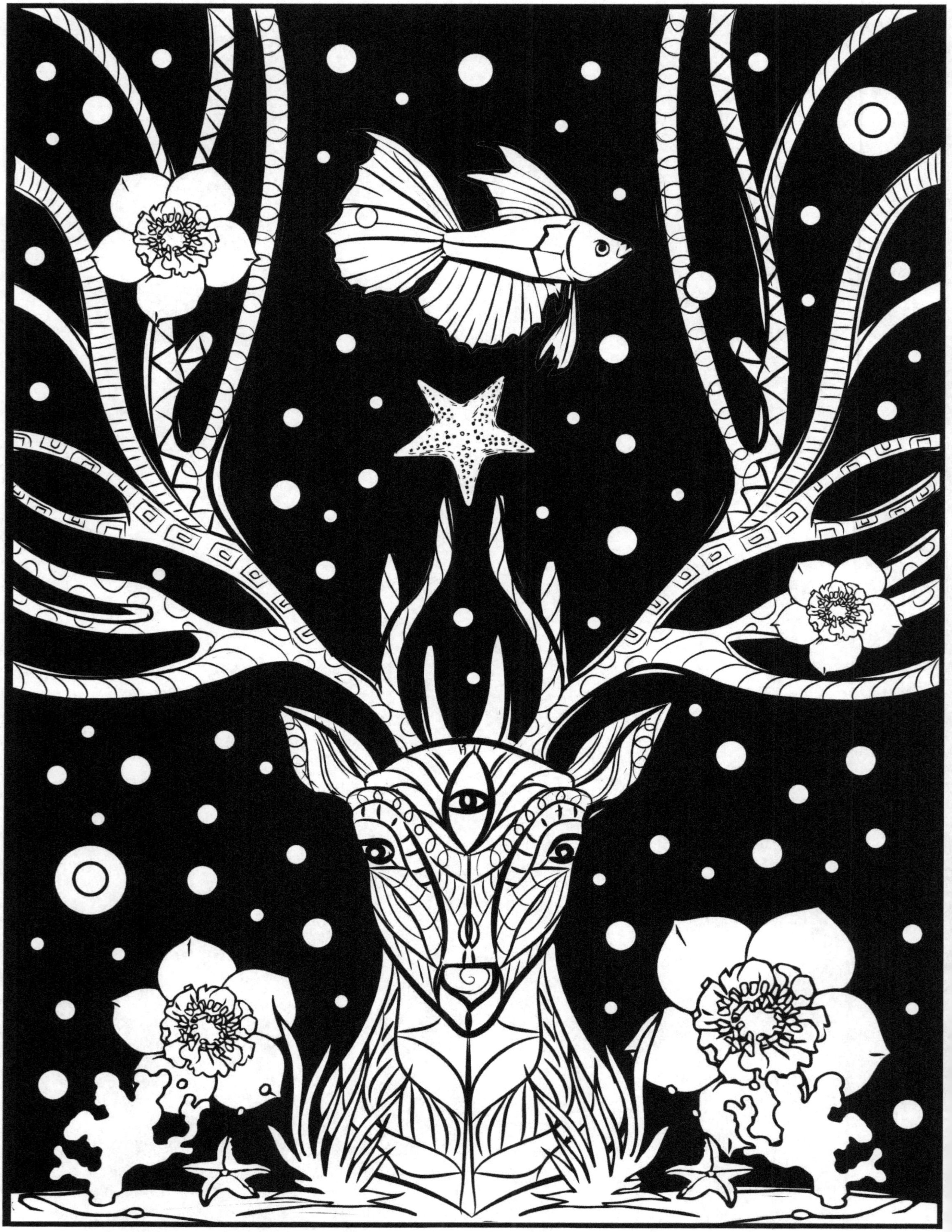

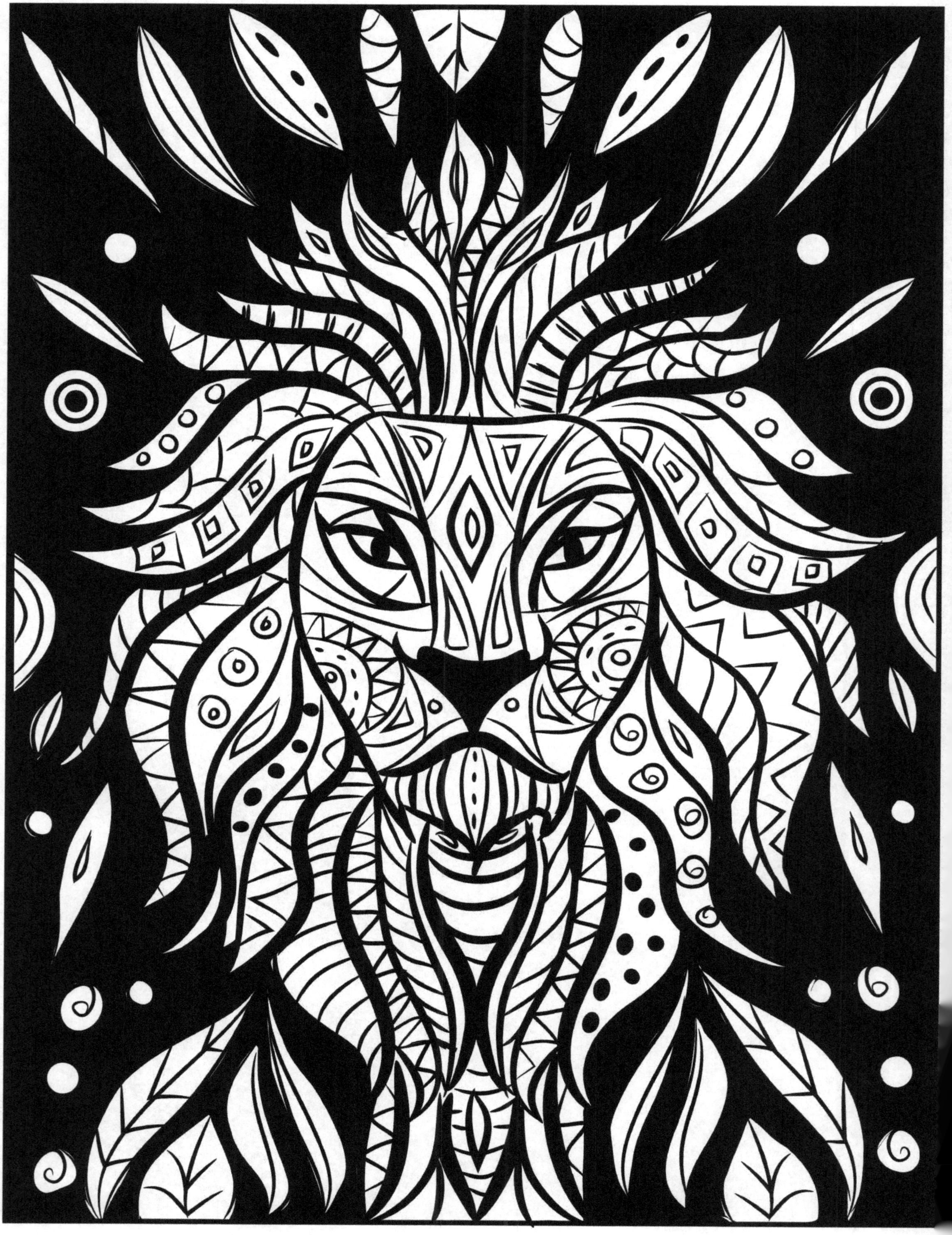

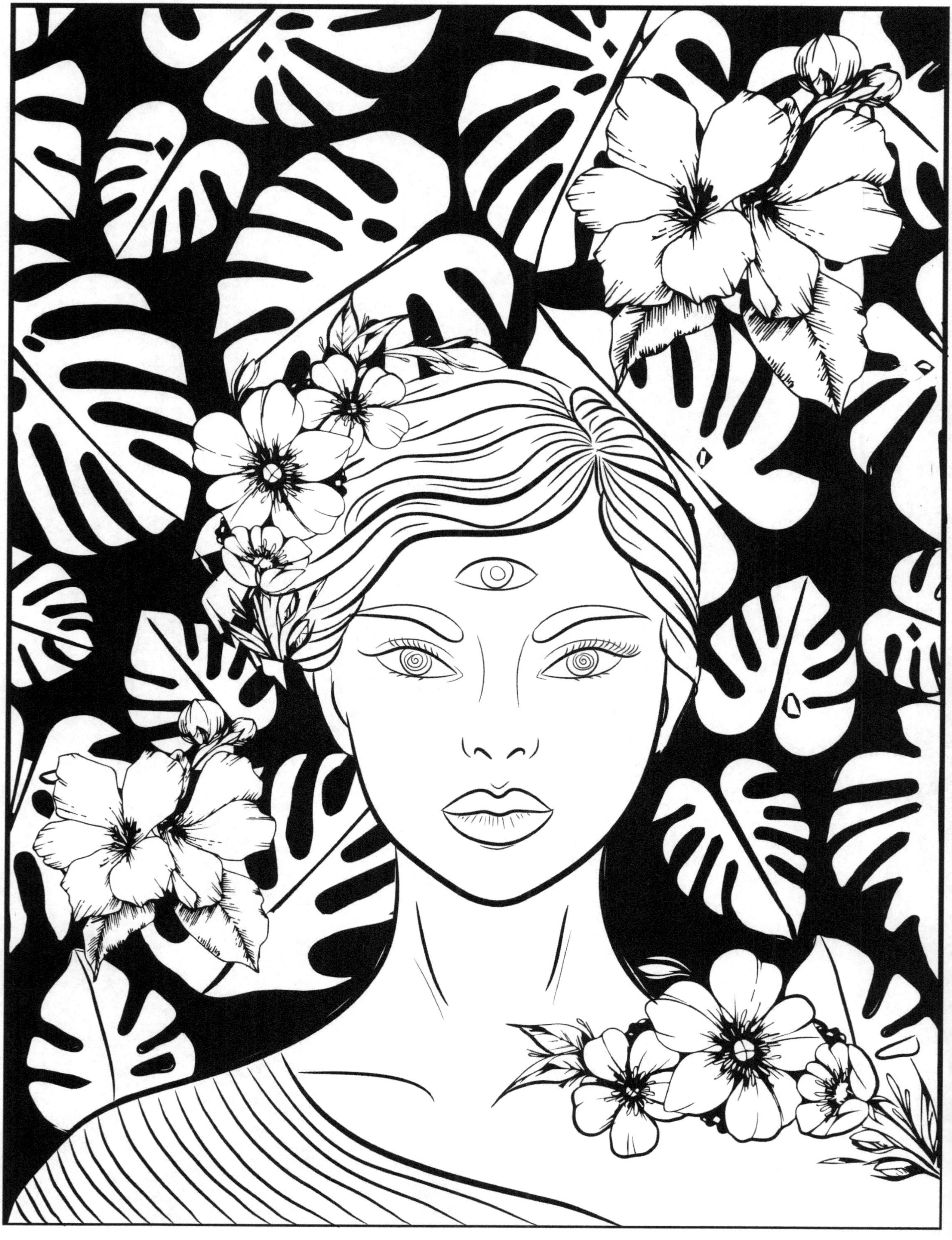

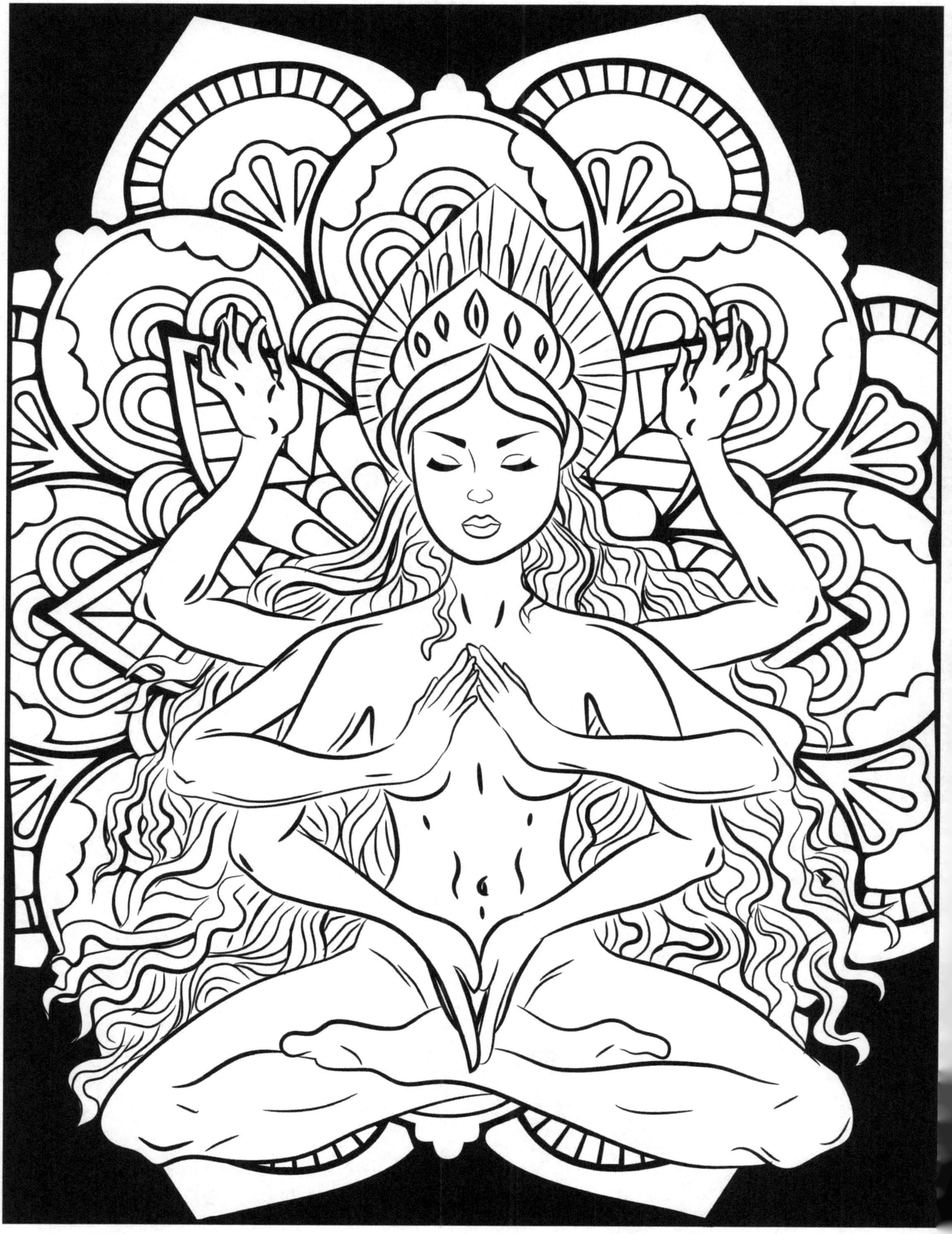

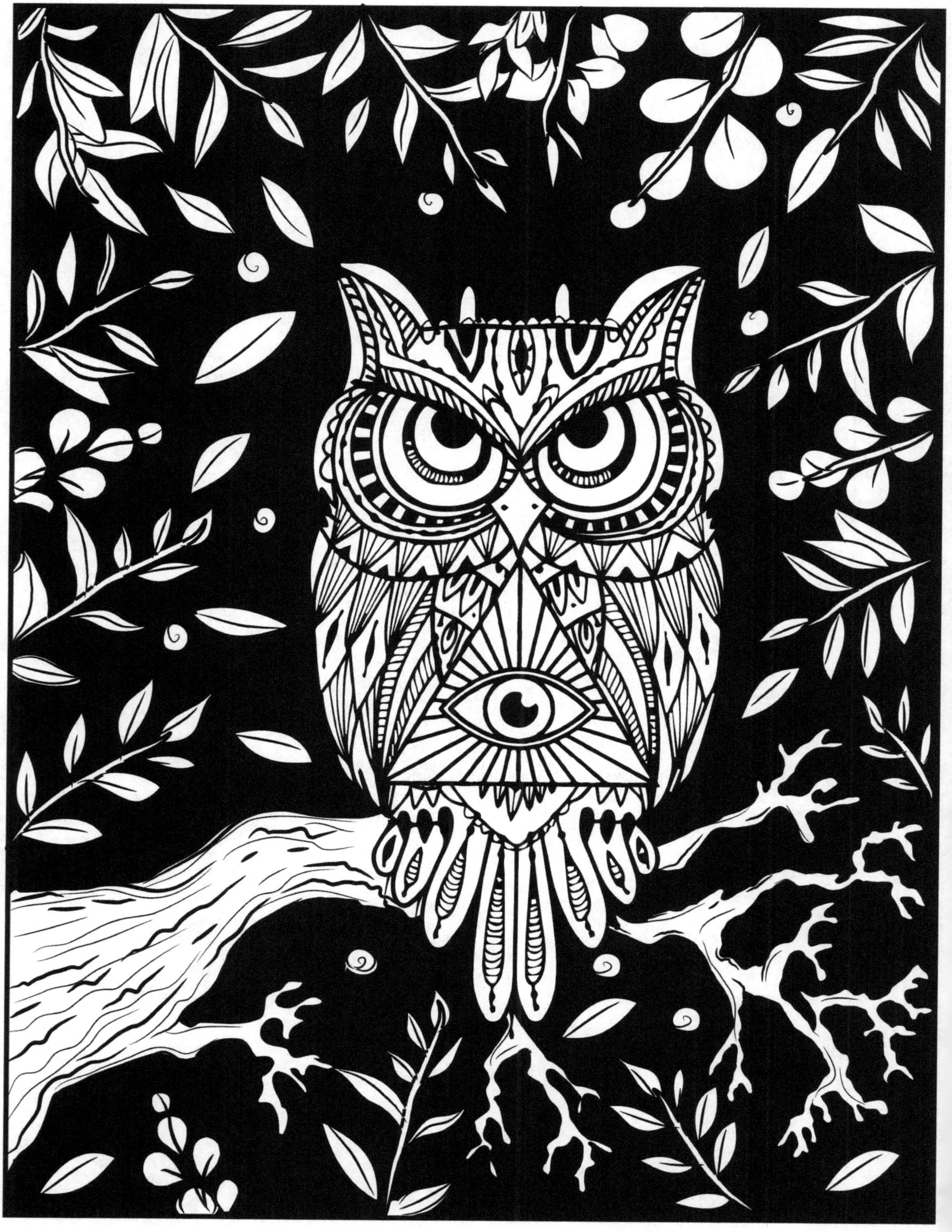

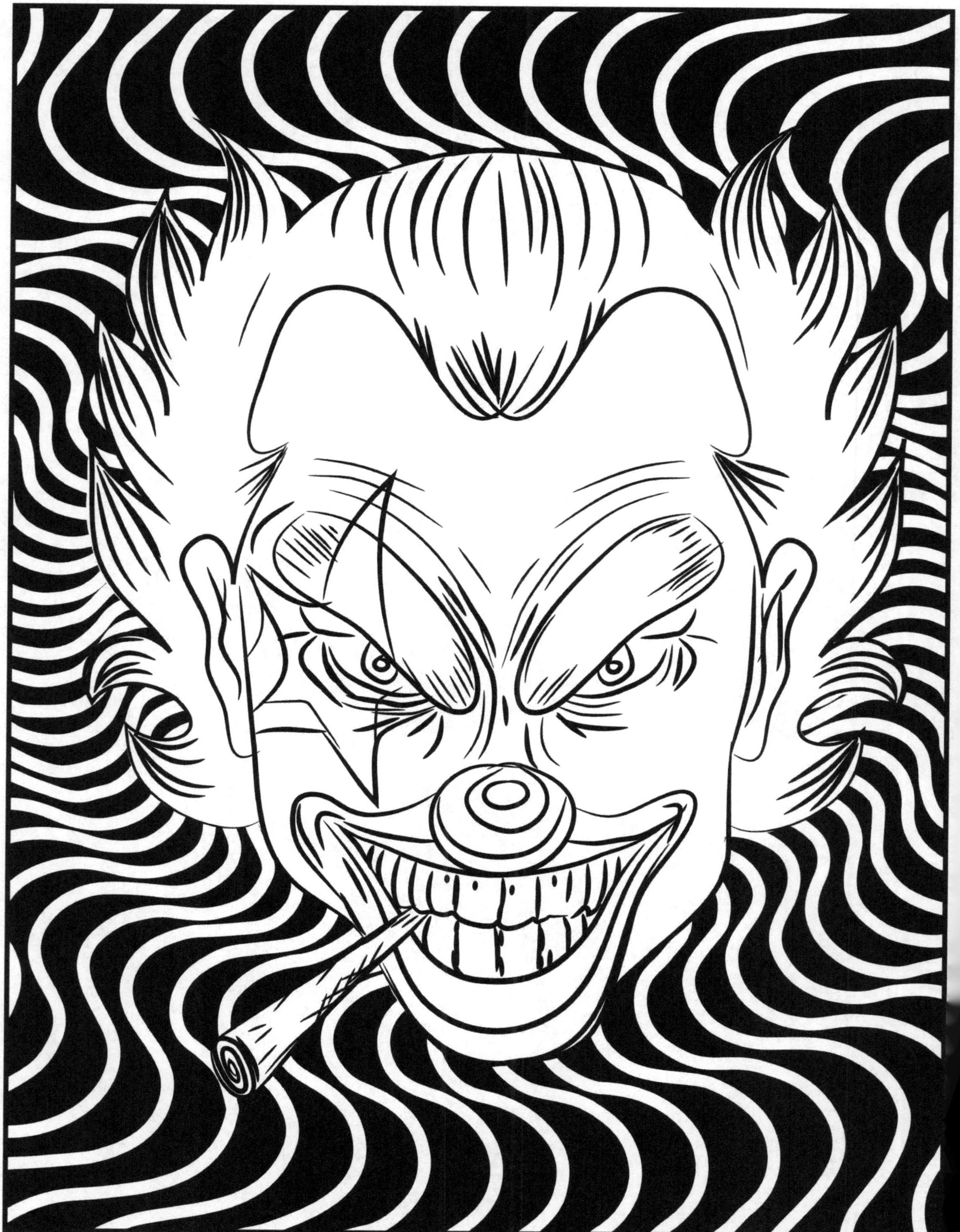

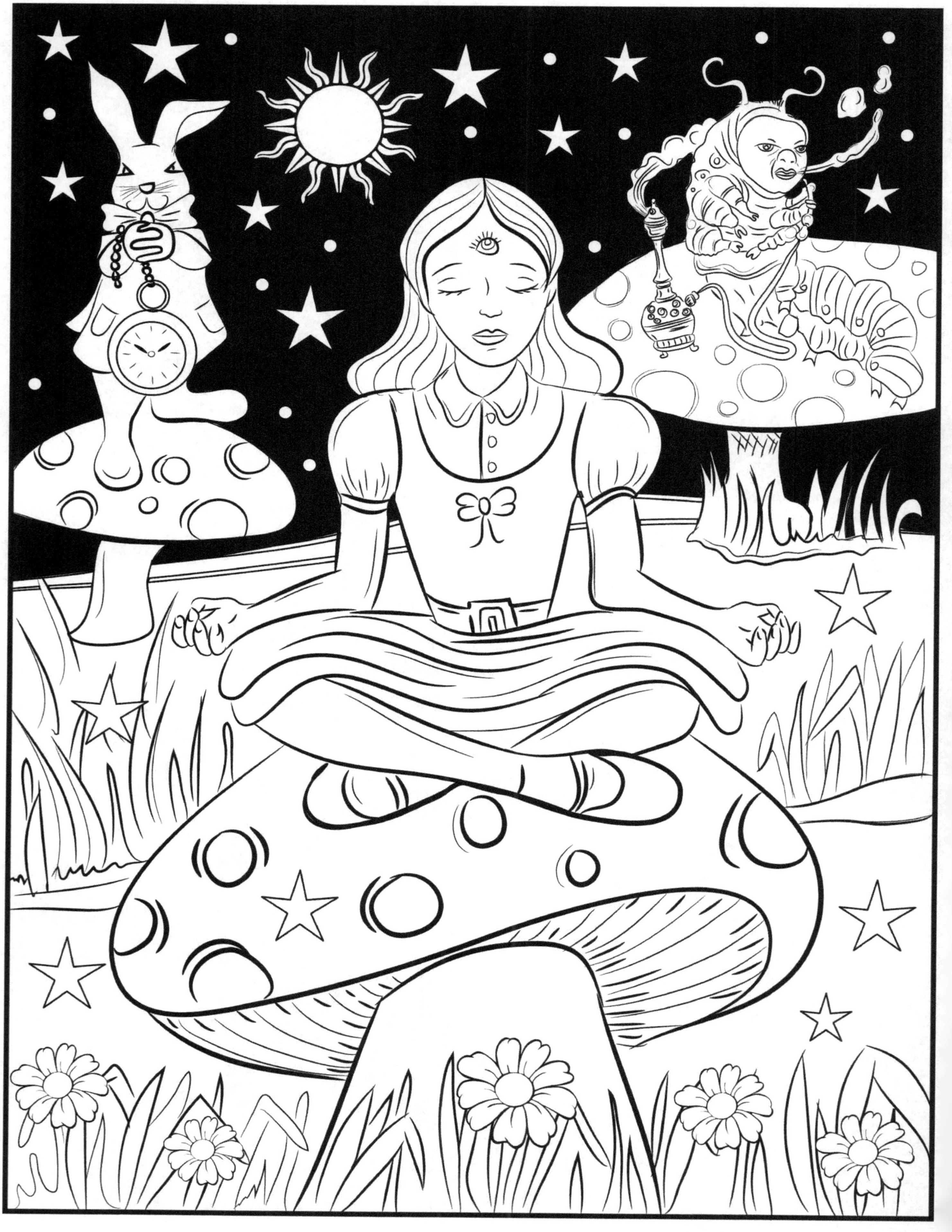

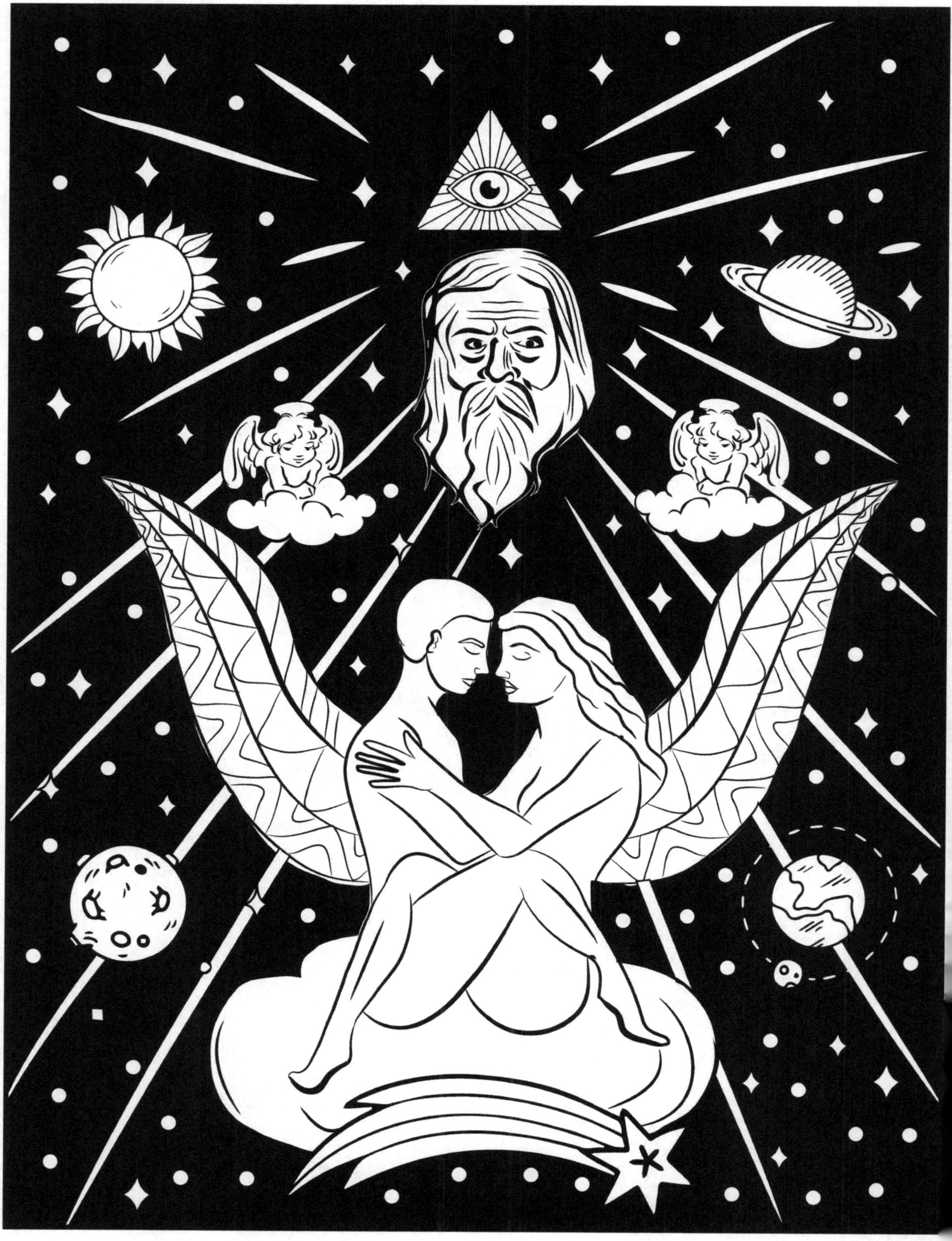

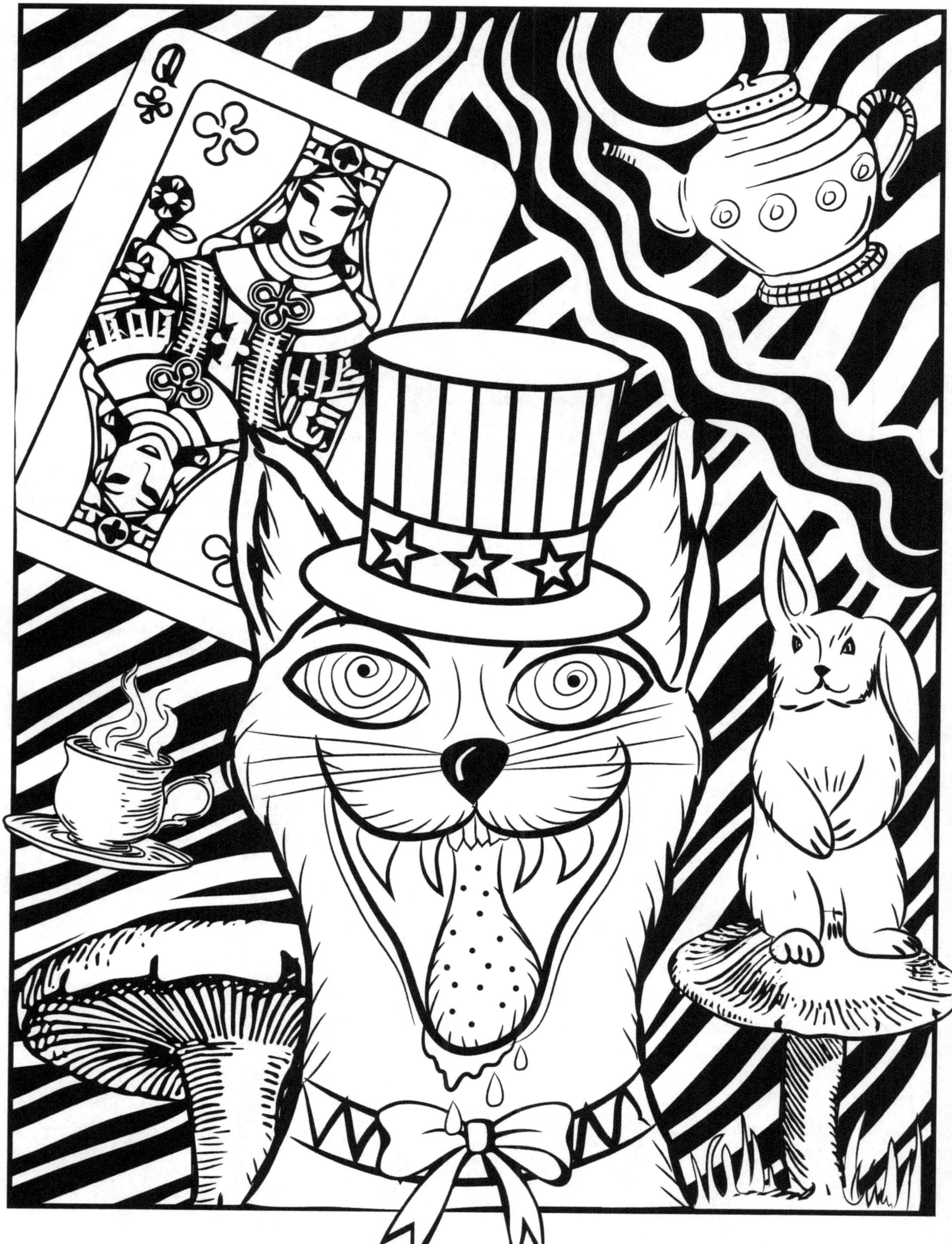

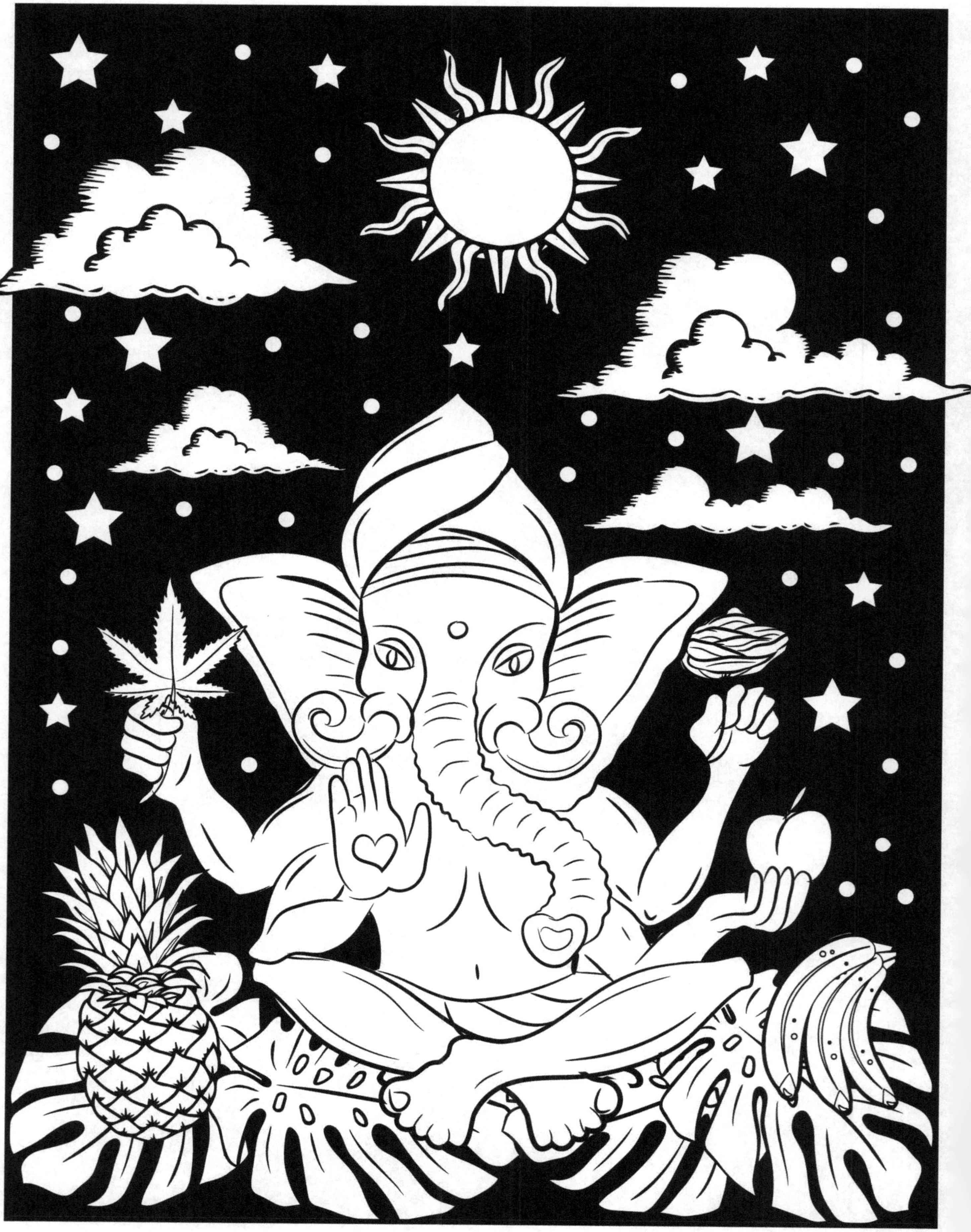

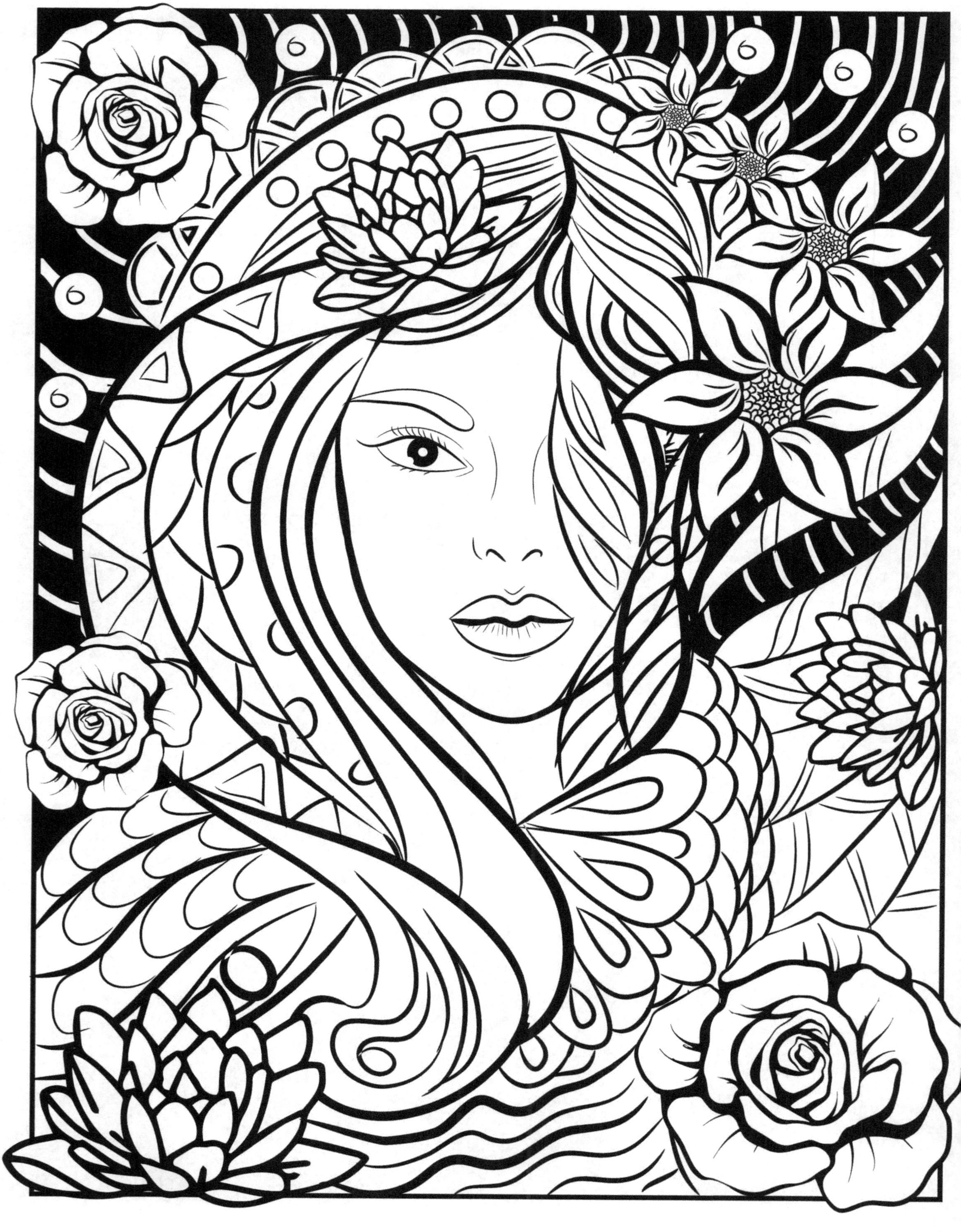

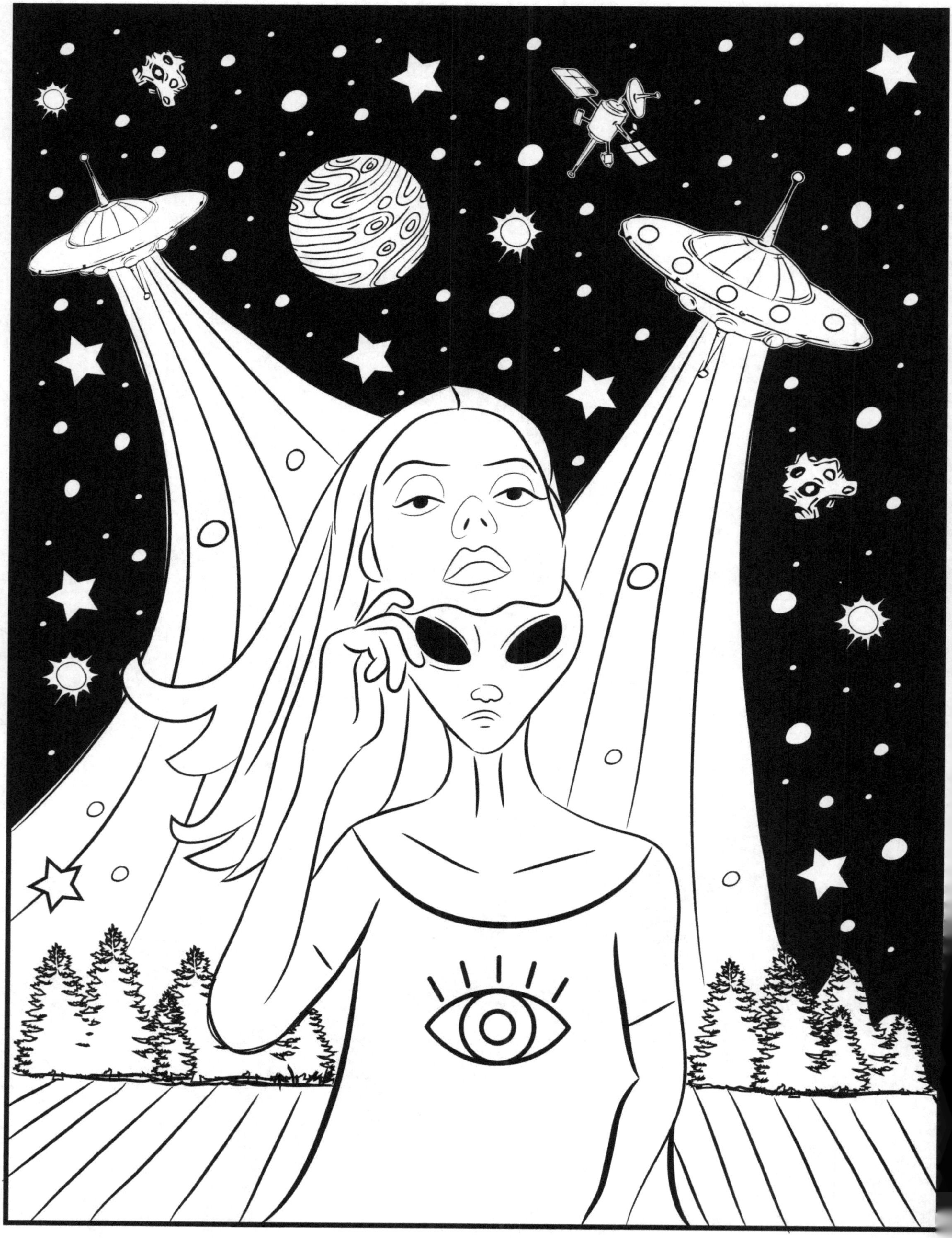

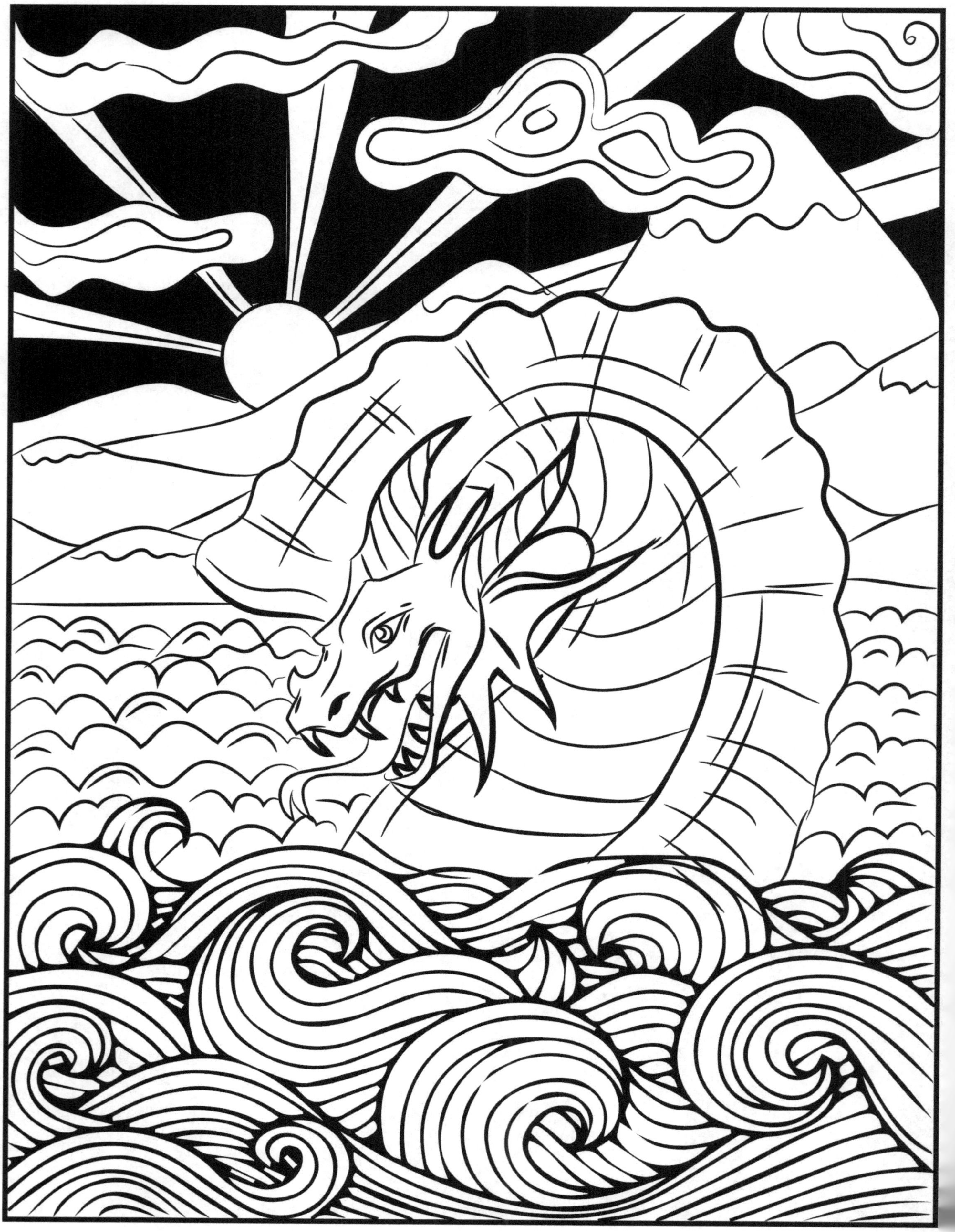

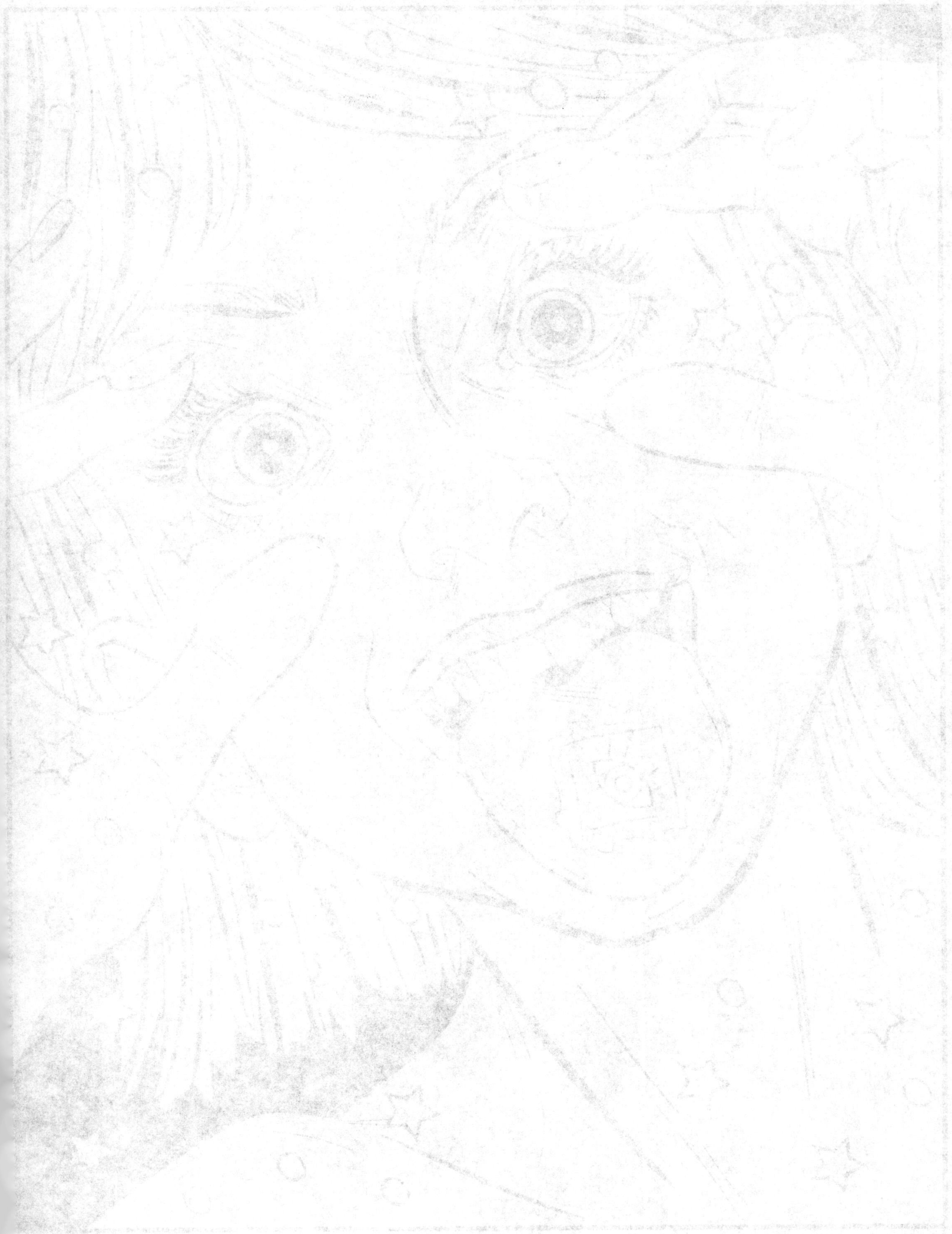

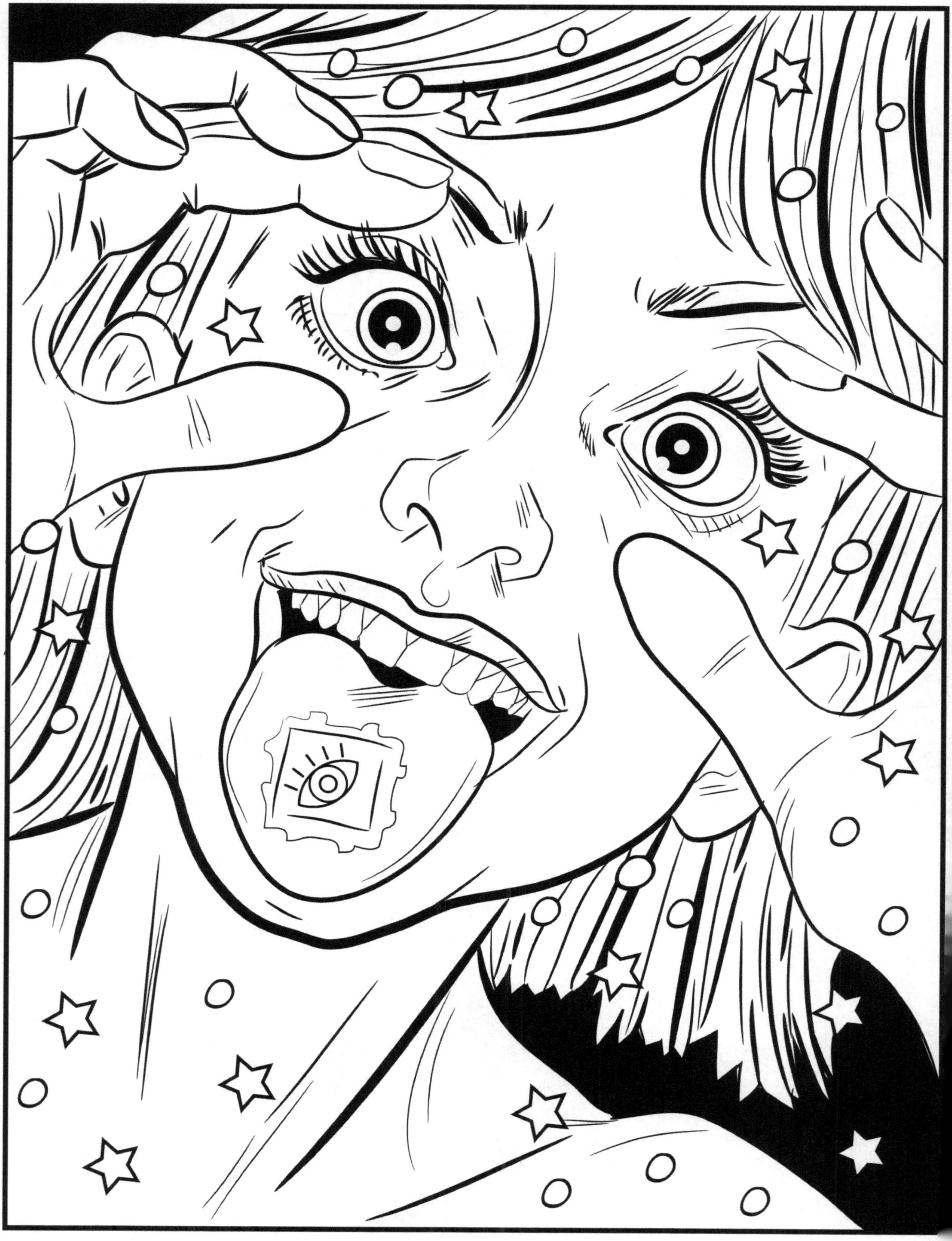

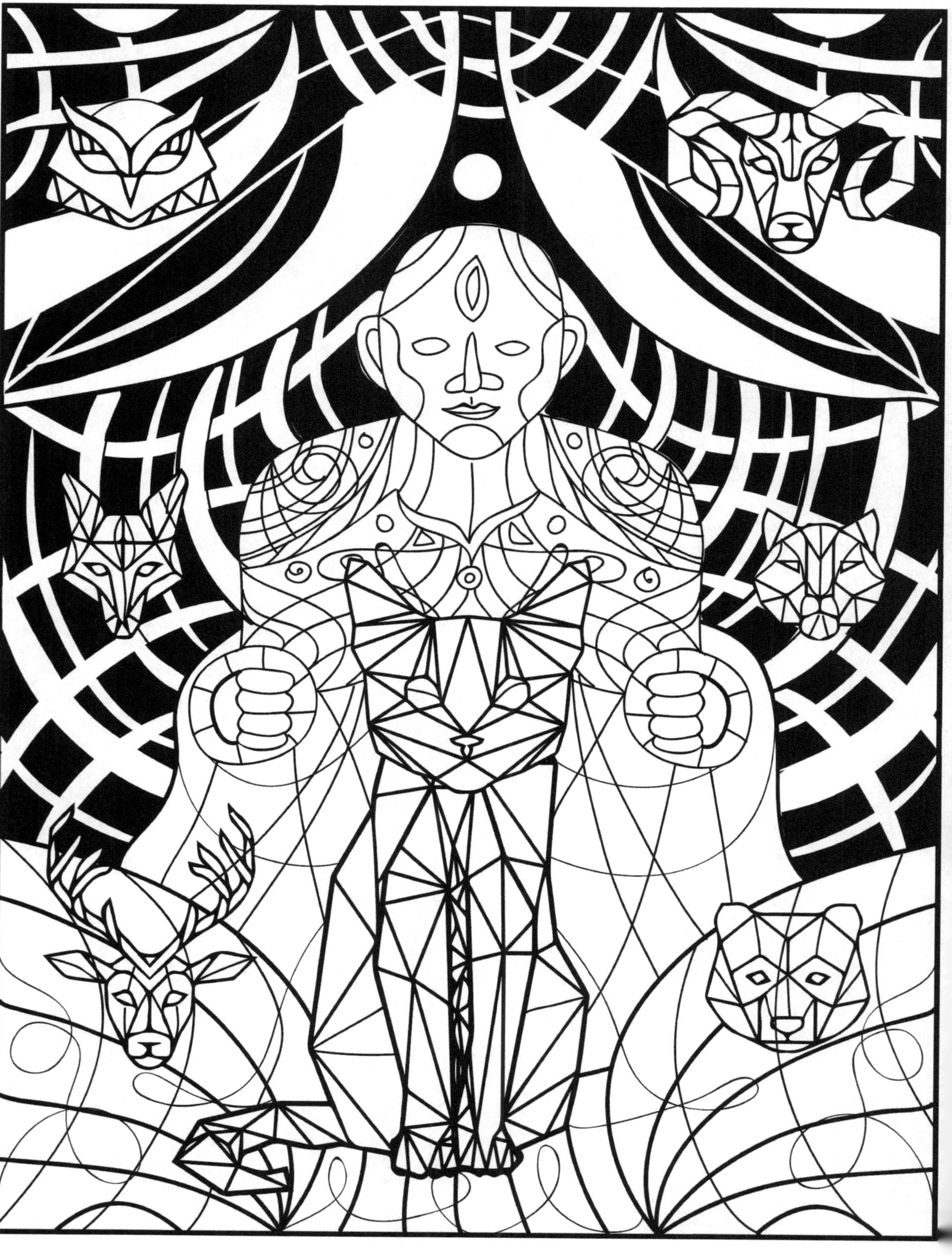

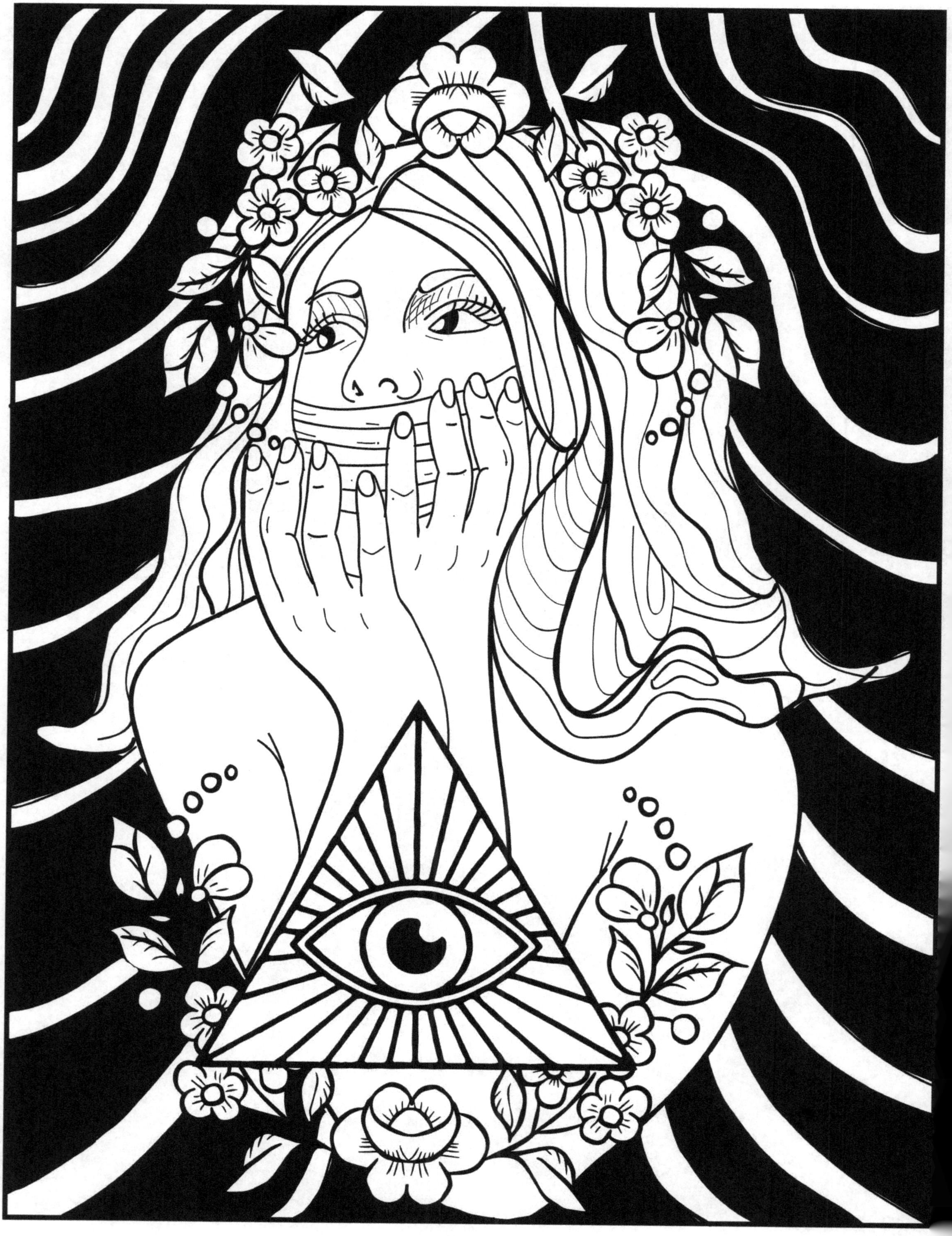

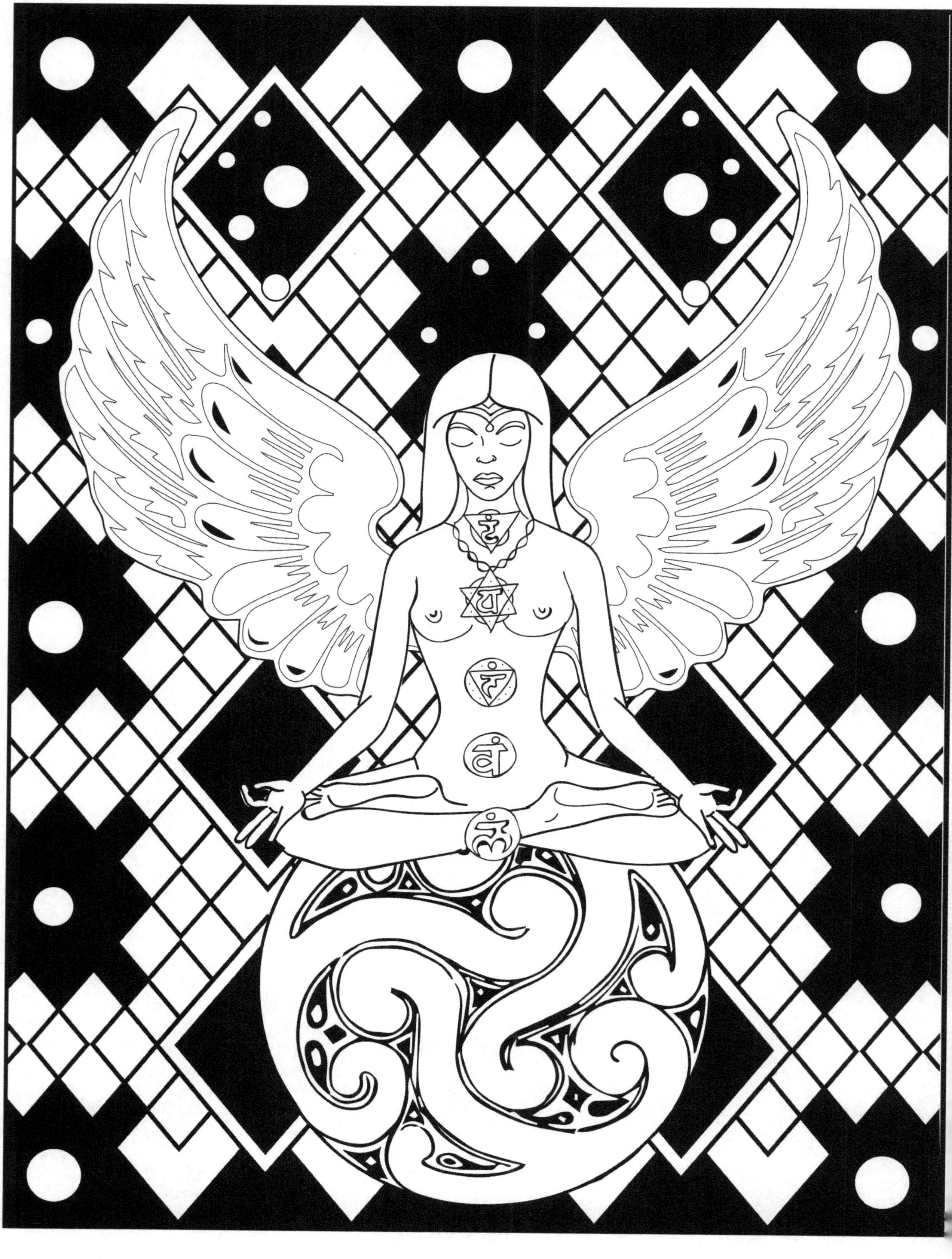

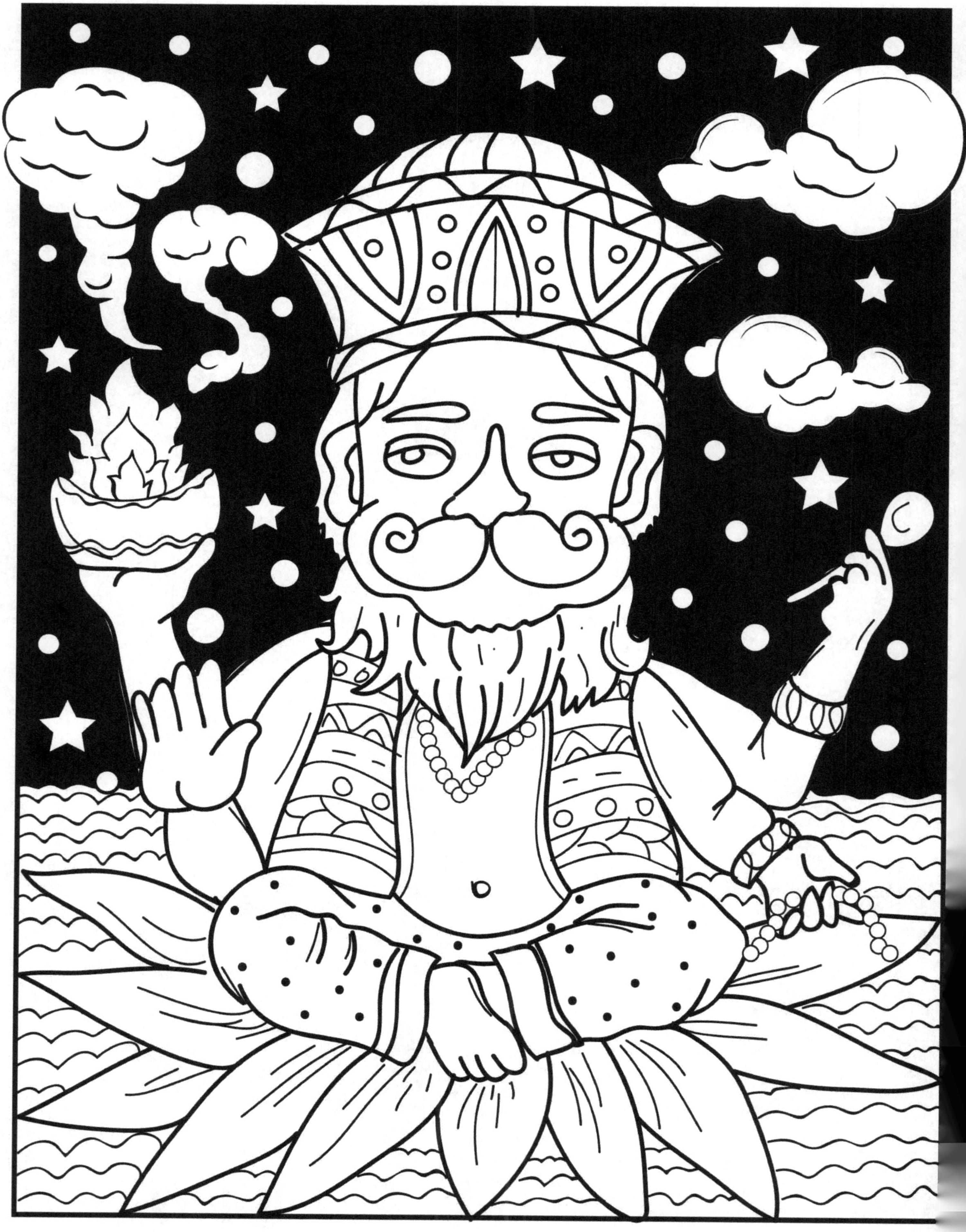

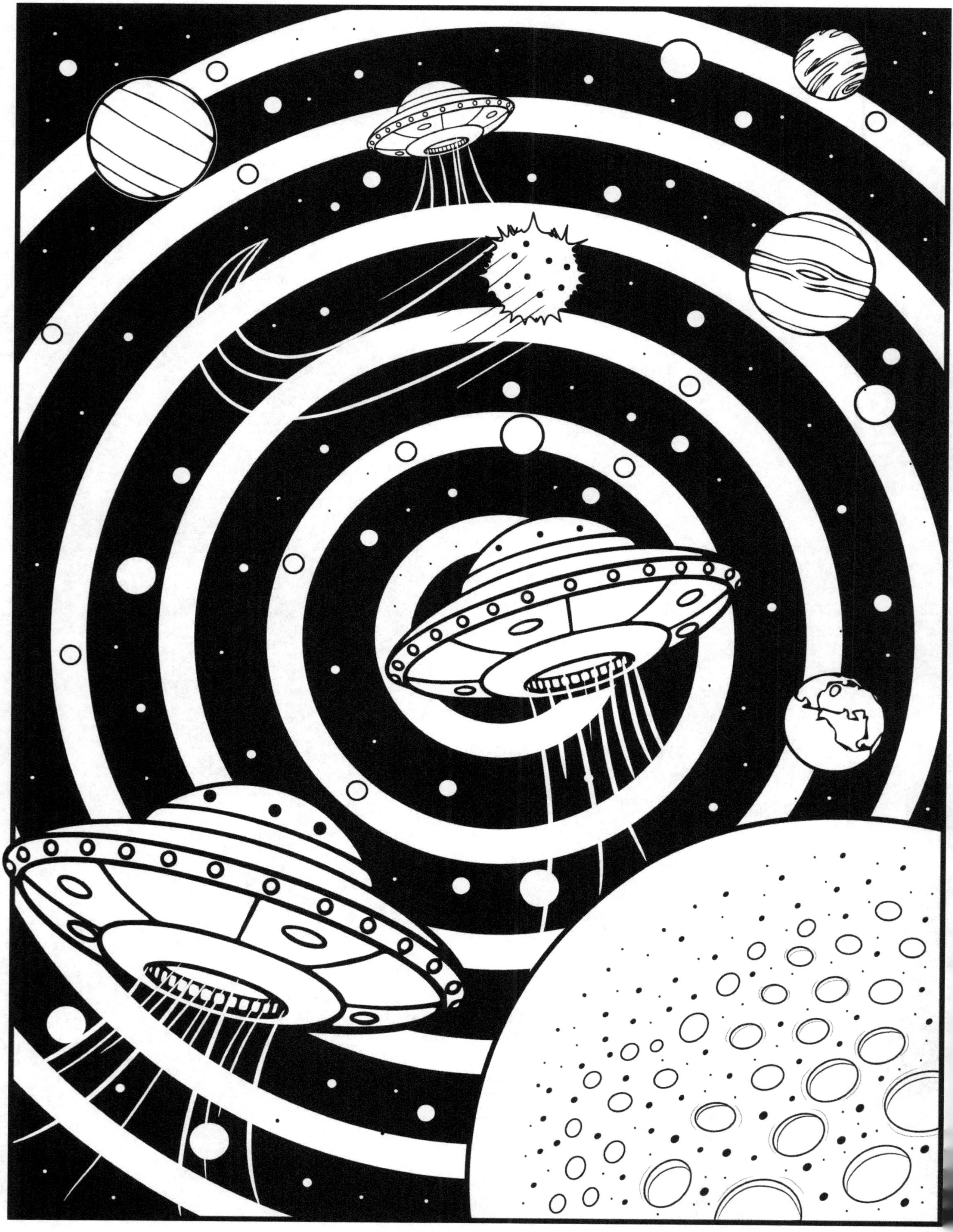

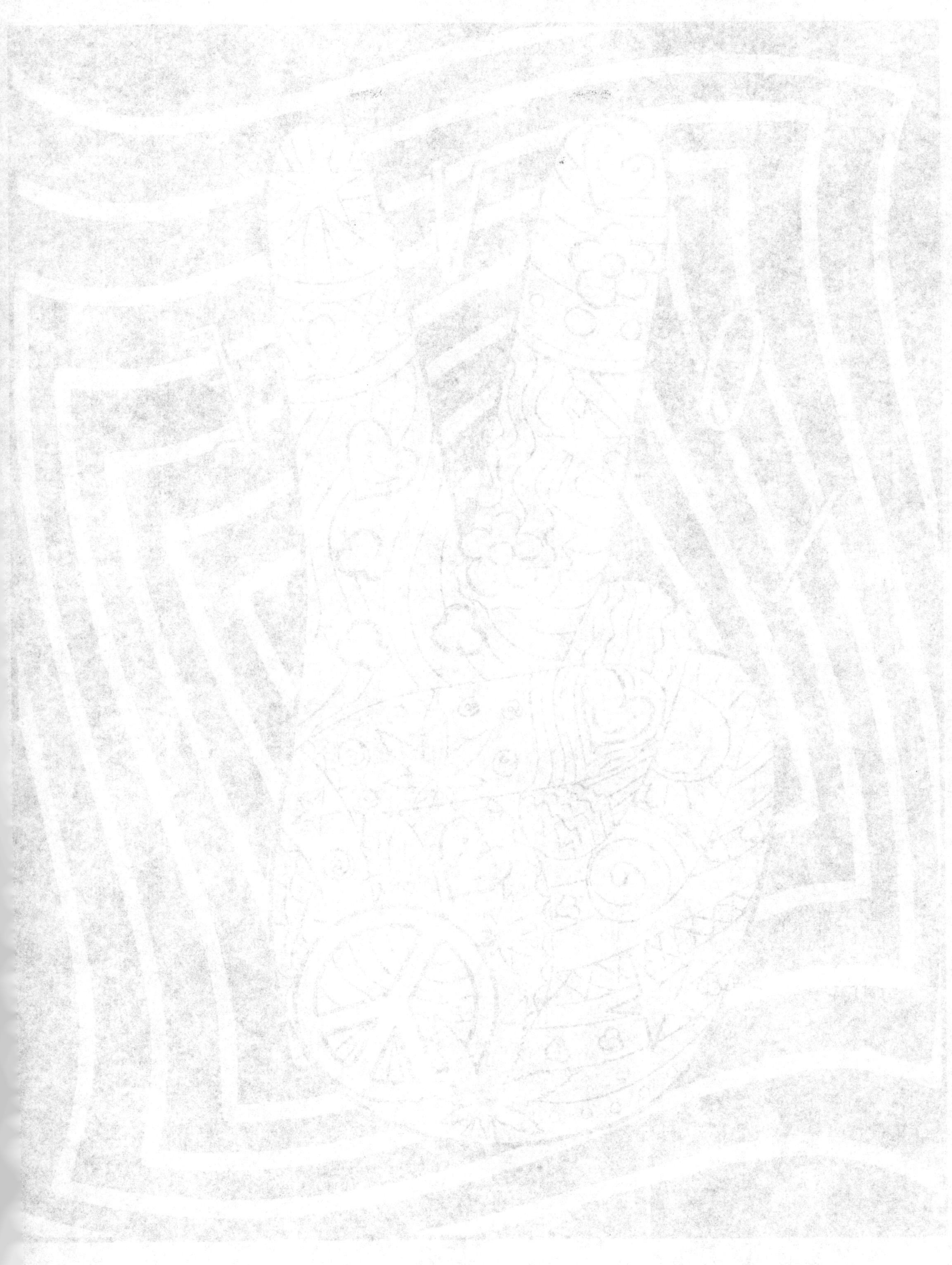

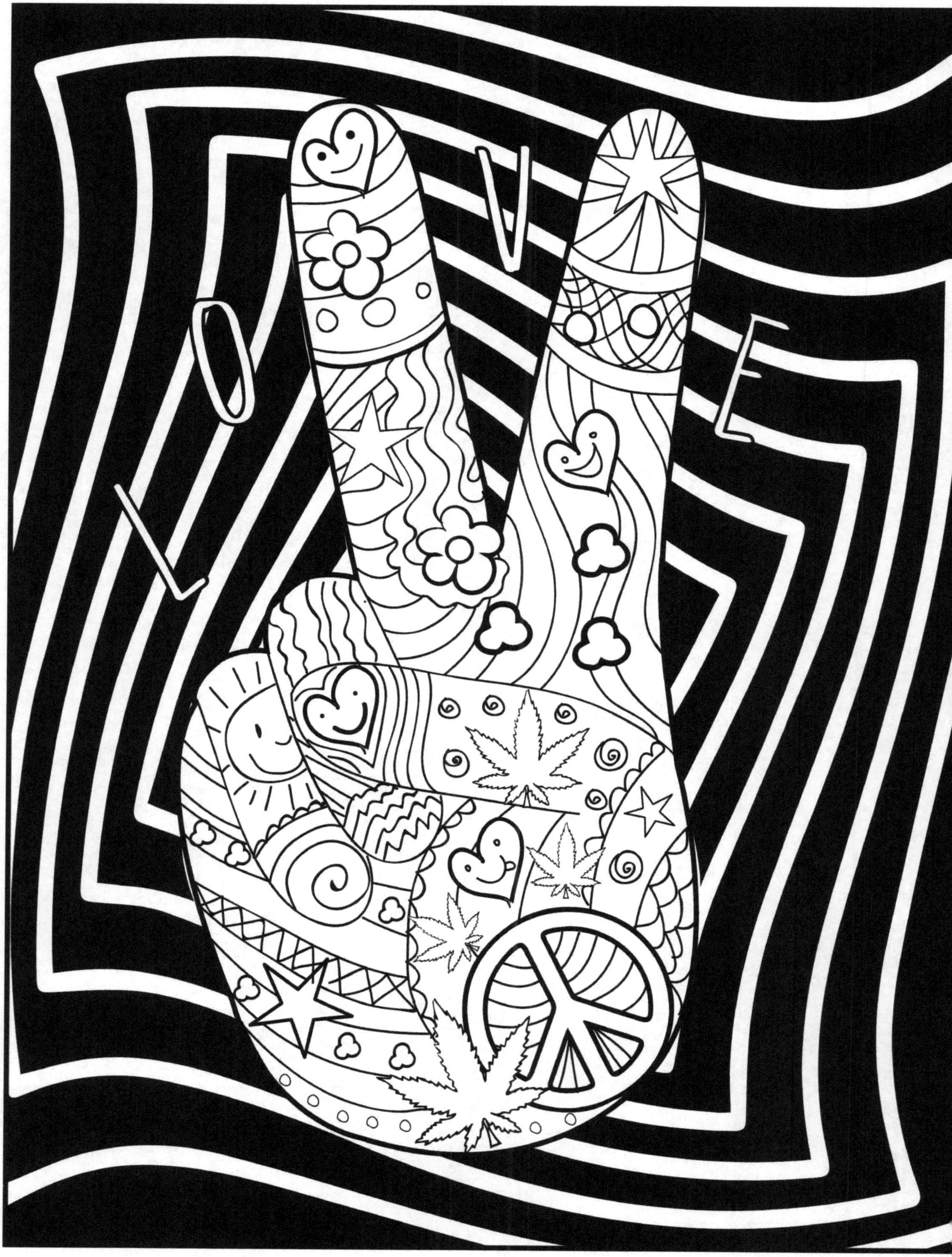
LOVE

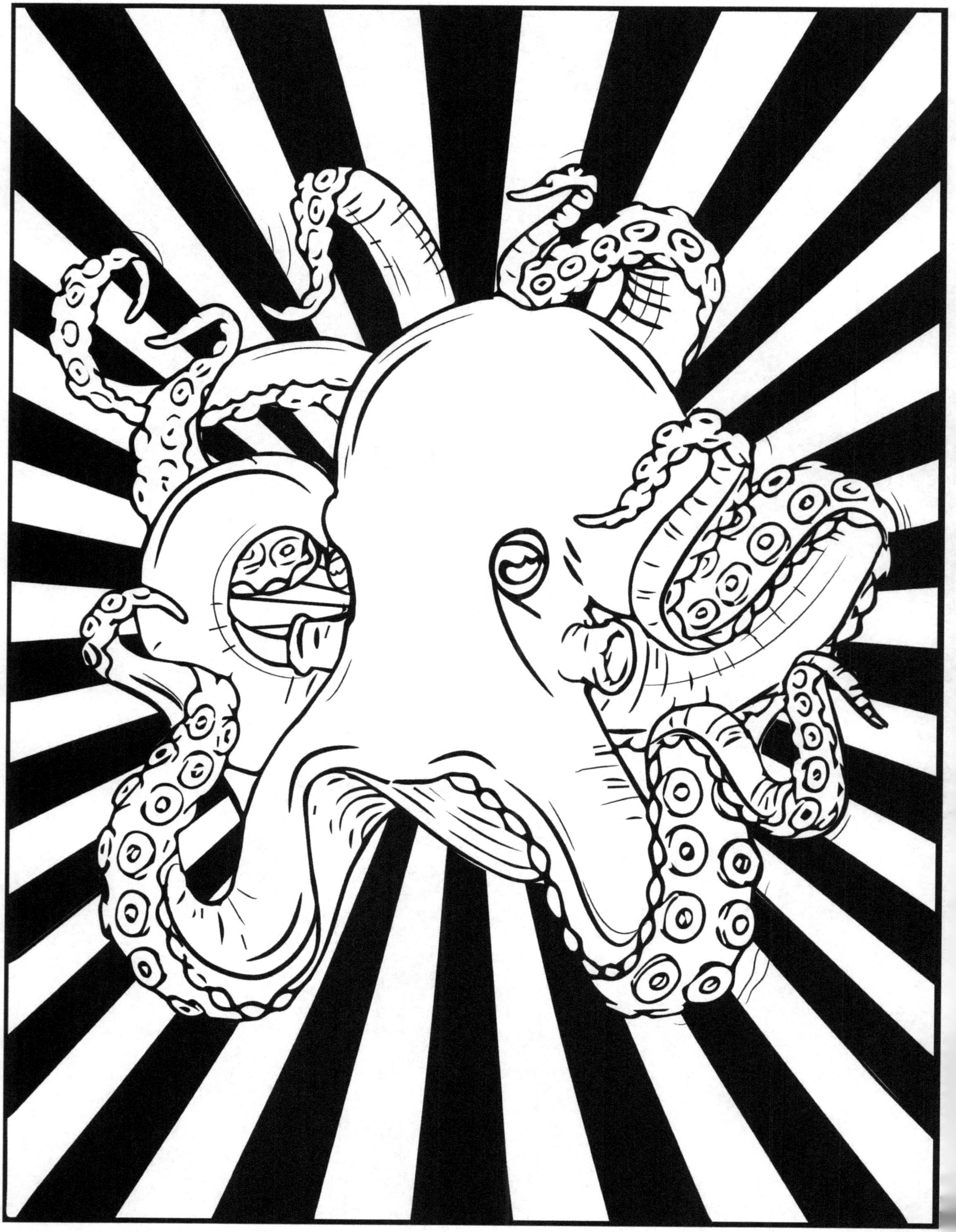

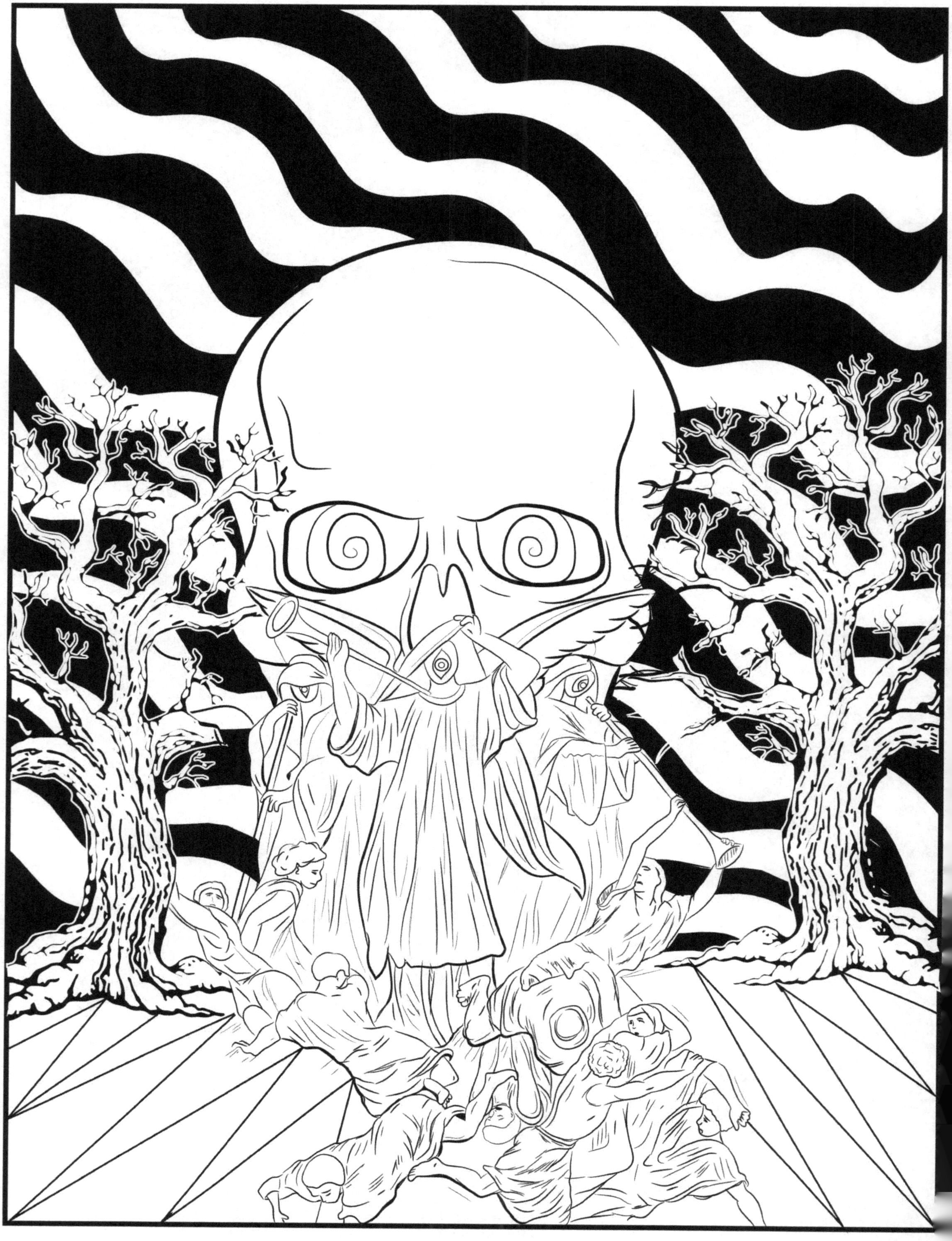

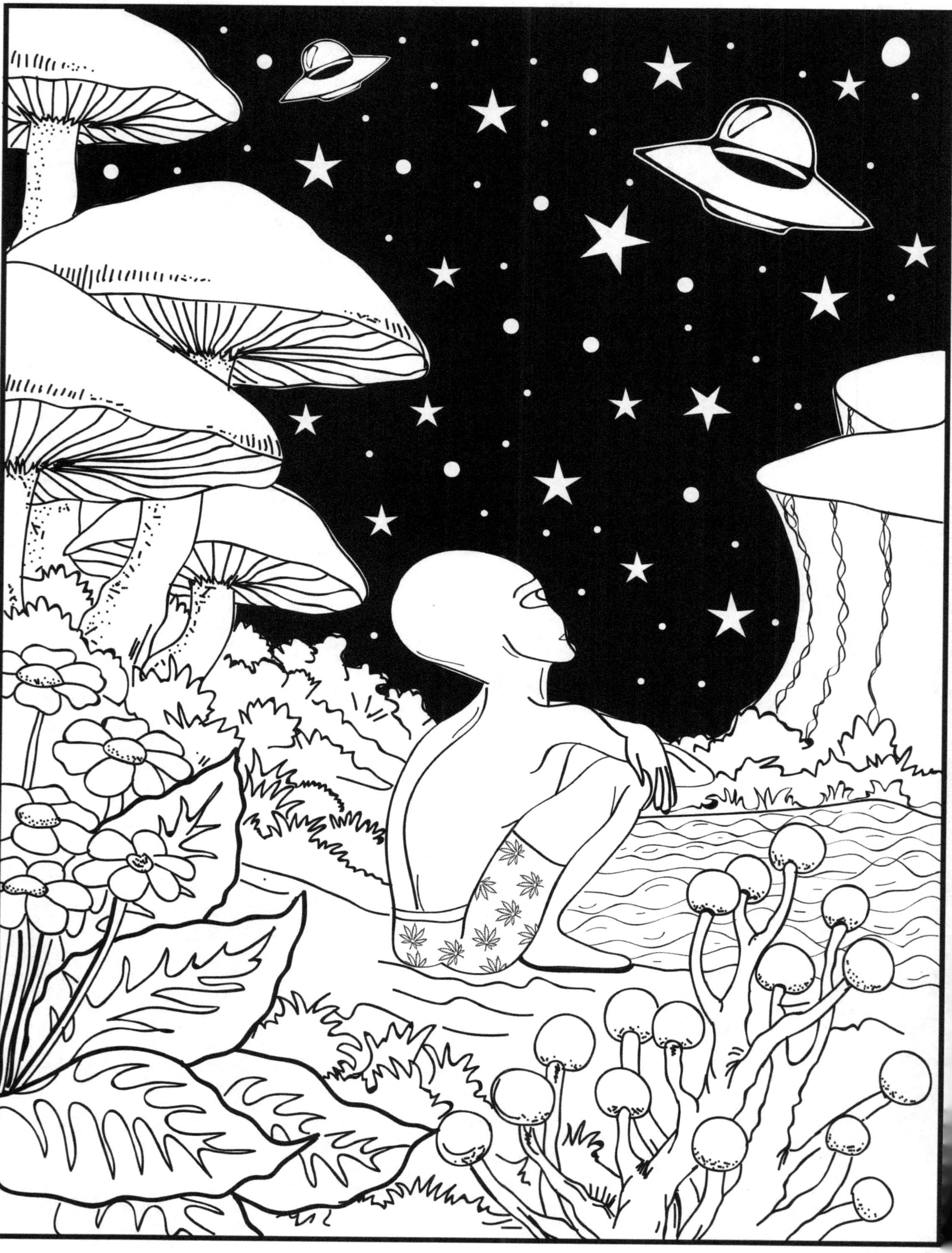

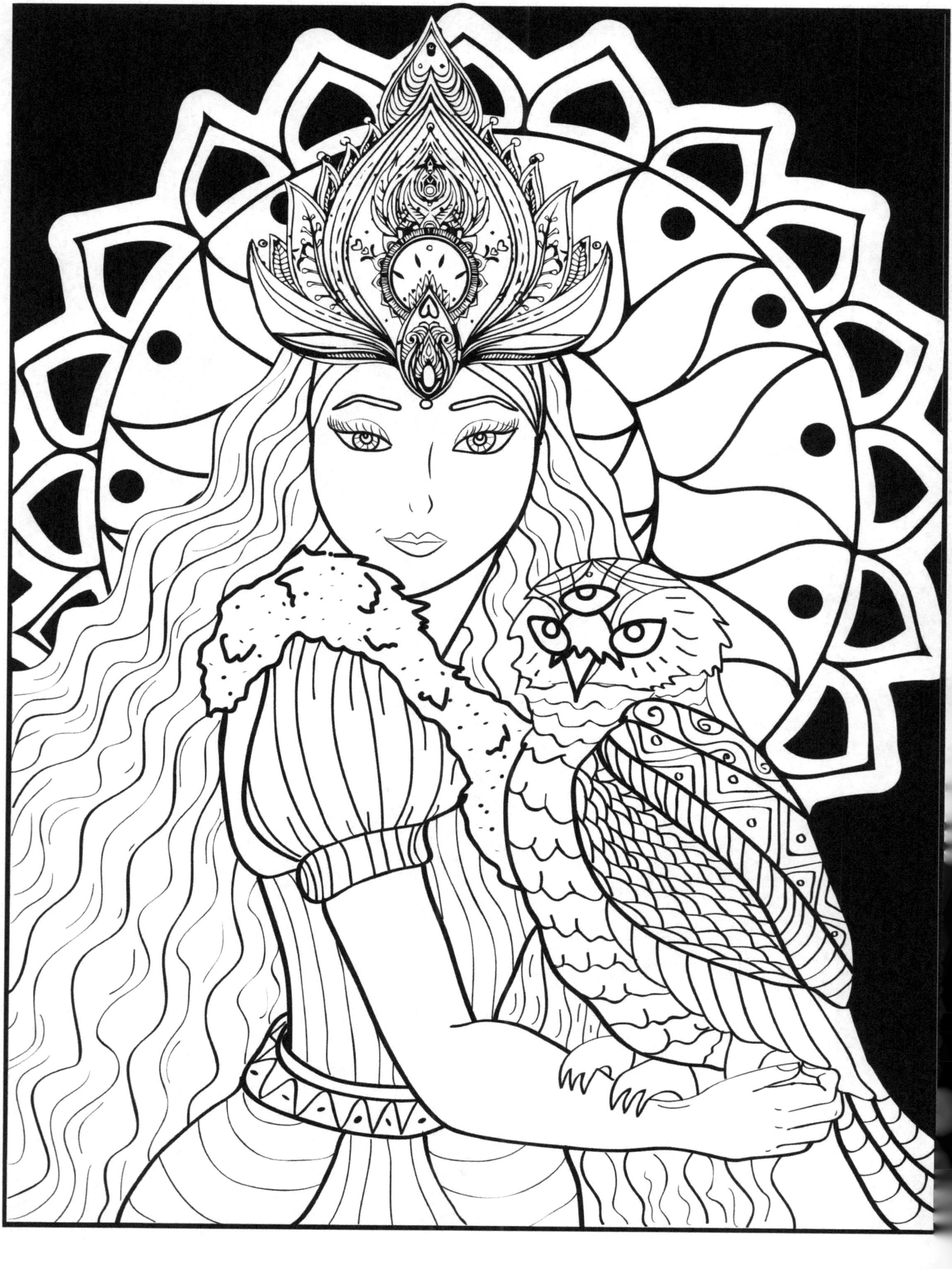

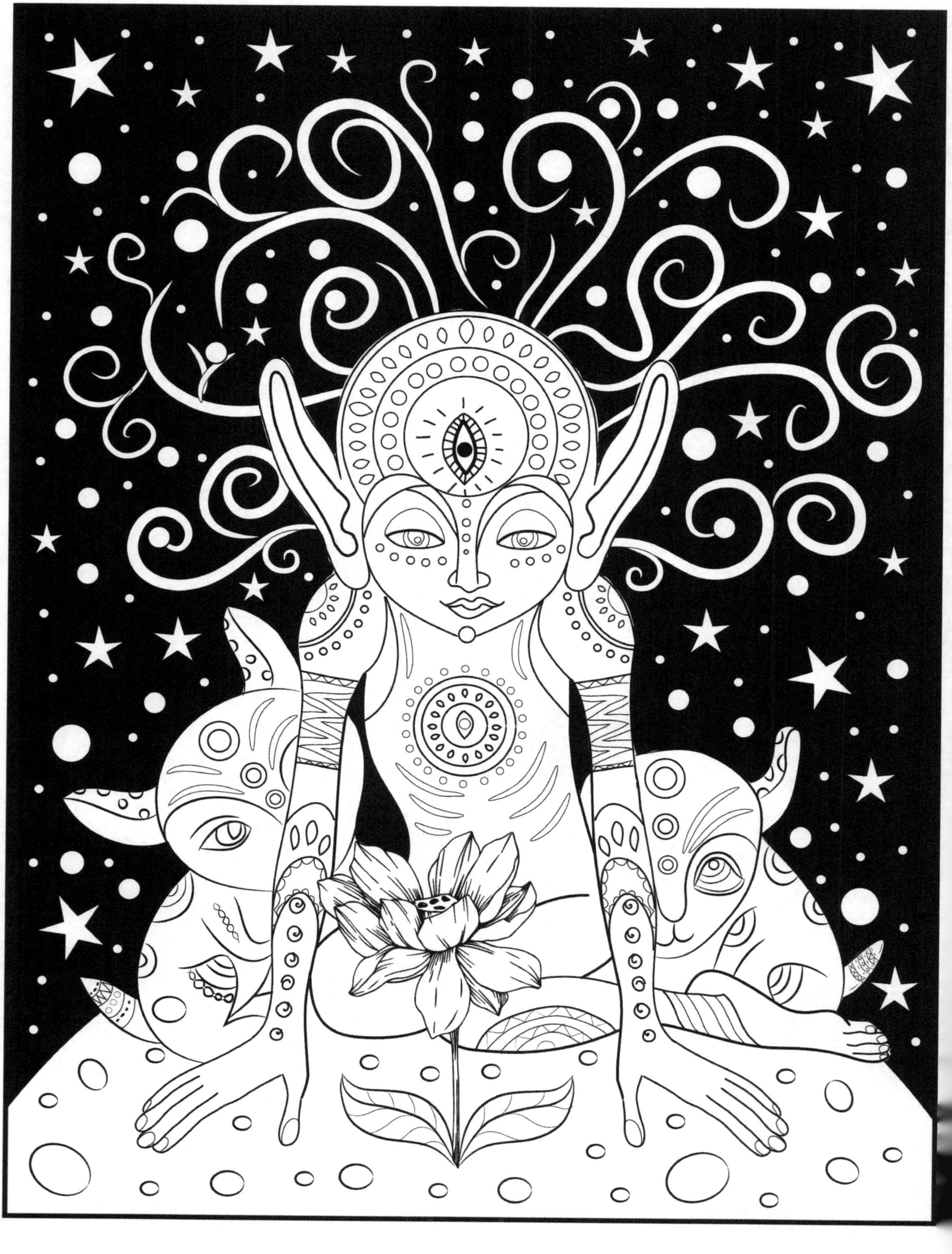

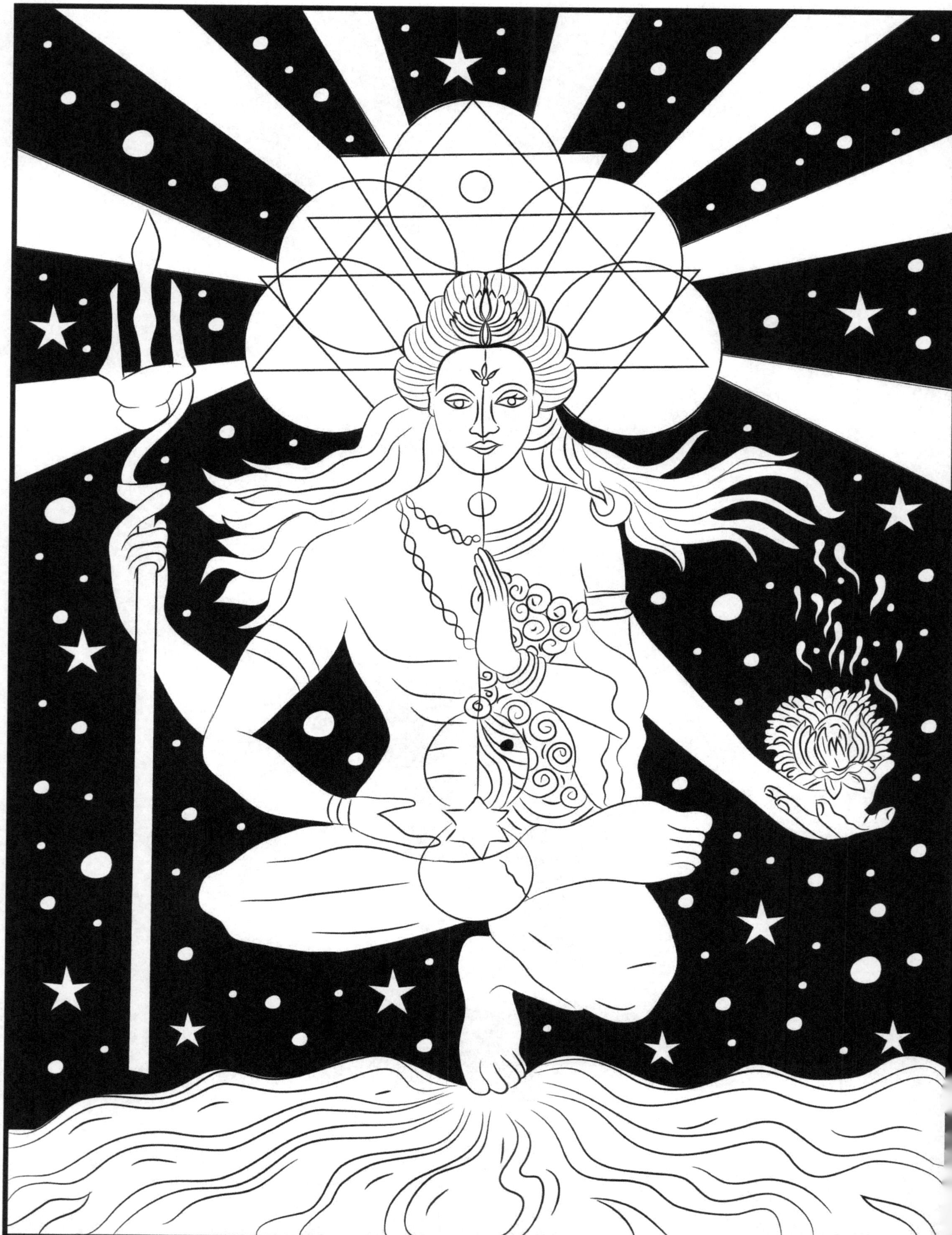

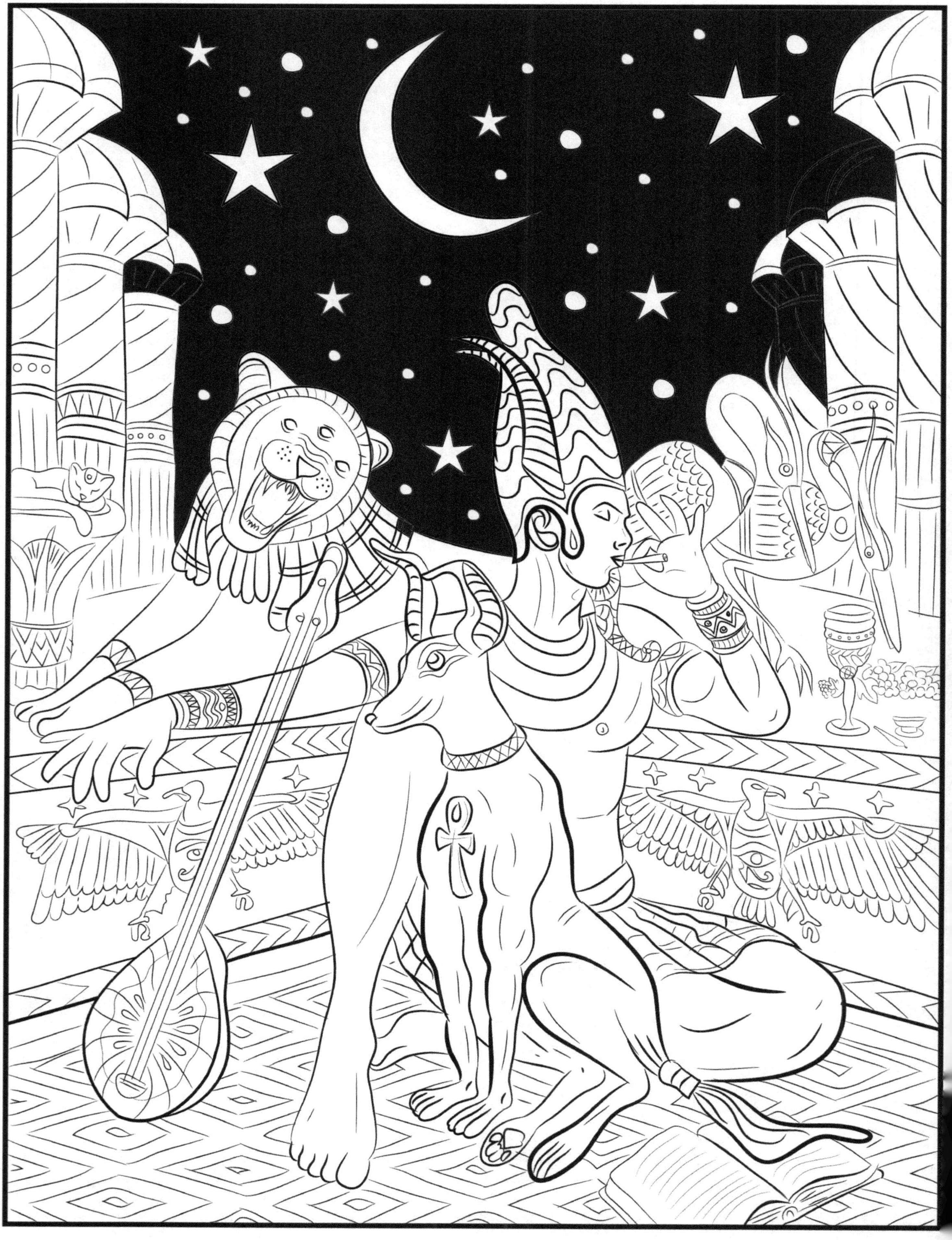

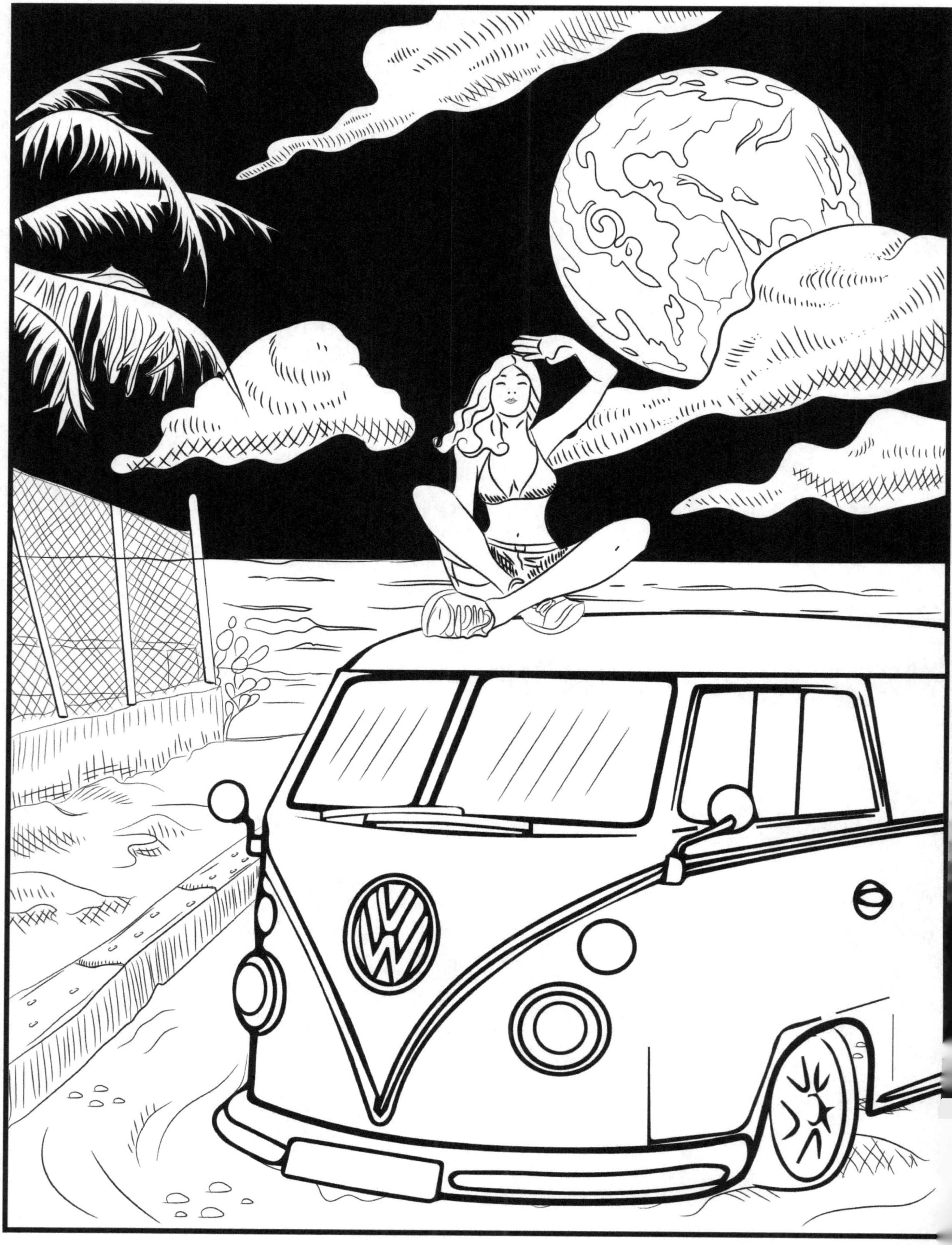

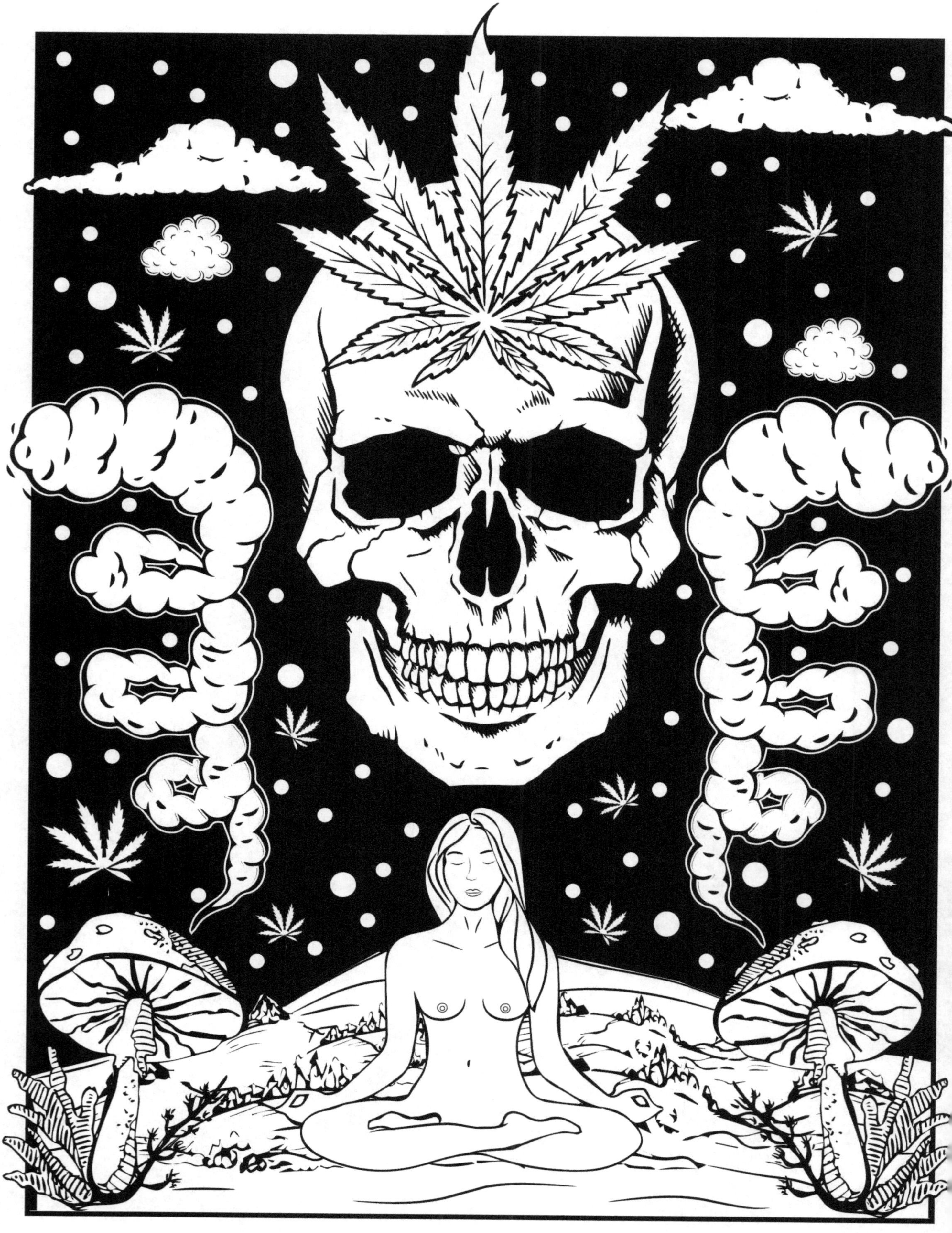

Did you enjoy the book?
It really helps out
small publishers like Nora
if you could leave a quick review
on Amazon.
Thank you in advance!
☆☆☆☆☆